THE WIFE IN THE NEXT LIFE

The Wife in the Next Life

ABEL KEOGH
JULIANNA KEOGH

**Abel & Julianna Keogh
The Wife in the Next Life**

Copyright © 2022 Abel & Julianna Keogh

All rights reserved. No part of this publication may be reproduced, stored in a retrieval system or transmitted in any form or by any means, electronic, mechanical, photocopying, recording or otherwise without the prior permission of the publisher or in accordance with the provisions of the Copyright, Designs and Patents Act 1988 or under the terms of any licence permitting limited copying issued by the Copyright Licensing Agency.

Published by: Ben Lomond Press

Interior & Cover Design by: Trevor Howard

Cover design copyright © 2022 by Abel Keogh

ISBN-13: 978-1-959945-01-7

BEN LOMOND
PRESS

This story reflects the authors' recollection of events. Some names and identifying characteristics have been changed to protect the privacy of those depicted. Some events have been condensed for literary effect.

For —

Hope
Aidan
Steven
Molly
Brennan
Brecklyn
Holden
& Ette

TABLE OF CONTENTS

Introduction 11
Chapter 1 Julianna.. 13
Part One Single Life.. 17
Chapter 2 Abel... 18
Chapter 3 Julianna 25
Chapter 4 Abel... 32
Chapter 5 Julianna 38
Chapter 6 Abel... 43
Chapter 7 Julianna 49
Chapter 8 Abel... 55
Chapter 9 Julianna 62
Chapter 10 Abel... 70
Chapter 11 Julianna 74
Chapter 12 Abel... 87
Chapter 13 Julianna 94
Chapter 14 Abel... 99
Chapter 15 Julianna 104
Chapter 16 Abel... 117
Part Two Dating Life... 124
Chapter 17 Julianna 125
Chapter 18 Abel... 138

Chapter 19 Julianna 149

Chapter 20 Abel 157

Chapter 21 Julianna 170

Chapter 22 Abel 178

Chapter 23 Julianna 187

Chapter 24 Abel 195

Chapter 25 Julianna 206

Chapter 26 Abel 211

Chapter 27 Julianna 217

Chapter 28 Abel 225

Part Three Married Life.. 238

Chapter 29 Julianna 239

Chapter 30 Abel 247

Chapter 31 Julianna 256

Chapter 32 Abel 263

Chapter 33 Julianna 271

Chapter 34 Abel 283

Chapter 35 Julianna 290

About Abel & Julianna 301

Acknowledgements 302

Other Books by Abel Keogh.. 303

INTRODUCTION

Sharing private experiences is difficult. The more personal the story, the more one is forced to acknowledge their mistakes, insecurities, and imperfections. We all want family, friends, associates, and coworkers, to see us without problems, concerns, or regrets. Social media is a prime example. Most people use these platforms to post photos, videos, and stories that make them look successful, happy, and virtuous. Rarely do people post something that show their flaws or failings. The truth is people are imperfect and complex creatures. That's why the best personal stories not only acknowledge one's blemishes but also show their endurance, faith, and courage even when the answers aren't forthcoming or the outcome unknown.

The Wife in the Next Life took years to write because it forced us to share our worries and weaknesses with the world. It addresses taboo subjects like polygamy, suicide, death, religion, and mental health. The project forced us to wrestle with questions and issues we thought we had dealt with years ago. It made us ask ourselves what we really believe and what is truly important in our lives. It was a demanding, time-consuming project but in the end strengthened our relationship and increased our faith.

For those who are struggling with the issues raised in the book or have similar concerns, we hope this book can help you find the courage to confront your questions and seek answers. For those who can't relate, we hope *The Wife in the Next Life* will give you more empathy and compassion for those who do.

— Abel & Julianna Keogh
December 2022

CHAPTER ONE

Julianna

When my fiancé, Abel, called me on the way to our wedding, I didn't hear the phone ring. I was mesmerized by the Bountiful Temple, a large, white granite building nestled in the foothills above Bountiful, Utah, a leafy, affluent suburb ten miles north of Salt Lake City. It felt surreal that I was going to be married in this beautiful building. Since I was a teenager, I had dreamed of marrying my future husband in this sacred setting, and in a few hours, that wish would become a reality.

At some point, I noticed a muffled ringtone emanating from the bowels of my small duffel bag. I reached inside and dug through the makeup, hairspray, gum, and other essentials before finding it.

"Who's calling?" my mom asked, turning to look at me from the front passenger seat.

"It's Abel."

My heart skipped a beat. *Why is he calling?* I checked my watch. We'd planned to meet at the temple in fifteen minutes. *Did something happen? Is he having second thoughts?* Worry and concern flitted about my innards like an overactive hummingbird.

"Are you going to answer it?" Mom asked, stalling my runaway thoughts.

Suddenly, I realized the minivan was quiet. The excited chatter from my three sisters in the back row had died down. My dad glanced at me in the rearview mirror, a questioning expression on his face. I answered the phone before it went to voicemail and steeled myself for bad news.

"Hey, sweetie. Where you at?" Abel said. His voice was happy and excited. I let out a breath and felt the tension in my body lessen.

"We're about to exit the freeway."

"Do you still want to get married?"

"I'm still planning on it if you are," I said, the uneasy feeling returning.

"That's great because I can't wait to be your husband," Abel said. "I'm leaving our place now. I'll see you soon."

Our place was a cramped, one-bedroom mother-in-law apartment four miles south of the temple. In the background, I heard a car door slam, followed by the vroom of an engine humming to life.

"I love you most times eternity," Abel said.

"I love you most times eternity too," I said, repeating our signature catchphrase. After we hung up, I exhaled in a deep sigh, somehow expelling all of the tension and anxiety packed into the previous thirty seconds.

"What did Abel want?" my mom said.

"He asked if I still want to tie the knot."

"Well, do you?" my dad said, a big smile on his face.

"Of course, I do," I said.

Laughter from my parents and sisters filled the minivan. I was too nervous to join in. Instead, I leaned forward to get a better view of the temple. In the morning light, its white façade stood in stark contrast to the brown, barren mountain.

I was excited to marry in the temple because Abel and I would be sealed in an eternal bond. That meant our marriage wouldn't end when we died, but would continue throughout the next life. Though an eternal marriage was the realization of a lifelong dream, there was one twist I hadn't planned on—my relationship with Abel might include his late wife, Krista, who had died fifteen months earlier. All morning I had pushed aside any thought of Krista, focusing instead on Abel and the new life we were creating together. But as we drew closer to the temple, concerns bubbled to the surface. Would Abel feel less excited being married the second time around? Would memories of Krista hang over his head as we promised to remain faithful to each other?

As I stepped out of the van, I spotted Abel walking across the parking lot toward the doors. When our eyes met, a smile stretched across his face as he hurried toward me. He greeted me with a kiss, then took my duffel so I could carry my wedding dress.

"You look gorgeous," he said.

"Thanks," I said, feeling the heat rise to my cheeks.

"You ready to do this?"

The bird-like feeling in my stomach returned, but instead of being accompanied by worry, it was combined with sweet anticipation. *I'm about to get married!* I pushed thoughts of Krista firmly from my mind.

"Yes," I said, taking his hand in mine. "I can't wait."

PART ONE
Single Life

CHAPTER TWO

Abel

On the computer monitor was a professional headshot of an attractive woman with straight, shoulder-length blonde hair, green eyes, and a million-dollar smile. Her name was Christine. According to her online profile, she was twenty-five years old, never married, and a semester away from earning a master's degree in Communications from the University of Utah. According to the dating website LDSsingles.com, she was my top online match.

I clicked the message button next to her photograph, and a box opened where I could type her a message. Instead of writing a note, I glanced over my shoulder, half expecting my wife, Krista, to walk into the room and, with a horrified look on her face, ask what I was doing. Krista wasn't there, but many of her things were. Against one wall, two bookshelves stood at attention, their shelves brimming with her books. Stacked neatly in the far corner were twelve cardboard boxes filled with what was left of Krista's personal possessions. Beyond them was an open door and an empty hall. The house itself was ghostly quiet—a pointed reminder that I lived alone.

Three months ago, Krista had taken her own life. She was seven months pregnant when she shot herself, and our marriage had instantly and unexpectedly come to an end. She wouldn't walk in on me today, tomorrow, or ever again. Despite this fact, browsing online dating sites overwhelmed me with guilt because I felt like I was cheating on her.

I returned my attention to the monitor and closed the message window. While guilt stopped me from sending Christine a message, it didn't prevent me from browsing the profiles of my other top matches. Maria, Nicole, Michelle, Heather, Stephanie, Lisa, and five others who lived within a twenty-mile radius of my home. All were in their mid-to-late twenties. Most had never married, two were divorced, and one was a single mother. None were widowed. For the next thirty minutes, I scrutinized their pictures, examined their profiles, and imagined a life together, punctuating each fantasy with a quick look over my shoulder to make sure Krista wasn't watching.

Even though I envisioned our dates and lives together in Walter-Mitty-esque detail, I didn't know if any of these women would even go out with a twenty-seven-year-old widower—especially one whose wife had passed away only three months earlier. If a date even happened, how would I explain to them why I was dating so soon? I foresaw conversations with future dates going something like this:

"Did you love your wife?"

"Yes."

"Did you have a good marriage?"

"Of course."

"Then why are you dating so soon after her death?"

It was a good question. I didn't have an answer.

The truth was, I had a strong desire to date. What I couldn't do was explain why I felt this way, where the feeling came from, or if it was even normal to want to date so soon after a spouse died. If I couldn't explain these feelings to myself, how could I explain them to someone else?

This desire to date had started about a month prior. When it first happened, I thought there was something wrong with me or that my feelings were a retaliatory reaction to Krista's suicide. I hoped the feeling would fade away. Instead, it became stronger. When I was out running errands and noticed an attractive woman, I checked to see if she wore a wedding ring, and if not, I thought of ways to start a conversation. The guilt that followed these fantasies was always thick and heavy, but it could never quite smother my longing for companionship.

For the last month, I'd looked for answers to my feelings without success. The so-called grief literature that was handed to me after Krista's death was for people over sixty. It focused on adjusting to living alone and making sure you had a good support network. There wasn't any information about starting a new relationship or the appropriate time between death and dating. Google, a new search engine that was touted by my tech co-workers as the best tool for searching the internet, didn't return any useful information either. My searches linked to funeral homes or grief boards—none of which I found helpful.

The adage that widowed folks should wait a year before dating was often repeated on these sites and in pamphlets, but I could never find a reason for that supposed rule or where that idea even came from. More than anything, I wanted to talk to a widower—preferably one who was young and remarried—about his experiences, but I couldn't find anyone who fit that description. Years later, I learned the desire widowers feel for a relationship is normal and some start dating days or weeks after their wife dies. But at the time, the lack of information on the topic made me think that there was something wrong with my wanting to date.

There were other options for finding answers. At least once a week, my mom suggested I see the same grief therapist she was meeting with. After each visit, she'd call and tell me how helpful the session had been and pass along booklets, handouts, and other resources the therapist had shared. I was glad my mom found the visits helpful, but her issues and mine were two different things. She was grieving. I wanted to date. Considering how much she was reeling from Krista's death, I didn't think telling her about my feelings was a good idea. That might result in even more therapy sessions.

There were also grief support groups that I might have attended if there was one specifically for widows and widowers. However, the descriptions contained words like "bereavement support," "grief loss," and "grief support," and appeared to be for anyone who experienced loss. I doubted I'd find answers to my dating questions among those who had lost children, parents, or close friends.

Despite not having answers, I continued looking for potential matches. Online dating was relatively new and had the stigma of being for people who couldn't get a date in real life. It was a perfect place for someone like me who, since Krista's death, felt like a social pariah. I'd been on the site less than a week, and today was the first time I'd thoroughly explored my online matches. Even though I was attracted to many of them, guilt stopped me from doing more than looking. Maybe tomorrow I'd feel different.

I was about to power down the computer when the thought came to search for widows my age. Maybe they wouldn't have qualms about dating a recent widower or would understand my desire to date again. At the very least, they could tell me if the guilt I felt was normal. If one of them had similar feelings, perhaps she could explain how to overcome them. With a fresh surge of optimism, I updated my search filters to look for widows under the age of thirty in a twenty-mile radius.

The results came back empty.

I expanded the search radius to fifty miles.

Nothing.

I tried one hundred miles.

Still nothing.

Giving it one last shot, I expanded the results to five hundred miles.

Zero. Zip. Nada.

I placed my head in my hands as feelings of frustration bubbled up inside. Was I the only widowed person in Utah under the age of thirty? That was impossible. Young people died every day from accidents, suicide, or illnesses. Some of them had to be married. But if there were other young widows out there, they weren't looking for love online—at least not in Utah.

Not willing to give up, I narrowed the search radius back to one hundred miles, but updated the criteria to search for widows under the age of forty. The site returned three hits. All three were in their late thirties. Two of them had four kids. The other had two children. None of their profiles said how long they had been widowed.

I wondered if the commonality of being widowed was enough to start a relationship. The death of a spouse, however, seemed like an odd thing to use as a foundation. Successful relationships are usually built on happy moments instead of shared sorrow. I thought about reaching out to the youngest of the widows, but realized that dating someone at least ten years older with children didn't appeal to me. I wanted to be a husband and a father again, but wanted to raise my own children. Things might be different if I was older or had living children of my own. Besides, if I was being honest with myself, I didn't know if I could marry someone who was sealed to someone else.

In The Church of Jesus Christ of Latter-day Saints, the faith to which I belong and believe, marriages don't end at death. If they take place in one of the faith's many temples, husbands and wives can be married forever—a process called "sealing" that allows marriages to extend into the next life. Knowing that family relationships can last beyond the grave is my favorite part of the faith. The knowledge that I could see and be with Krista again is comforting. However, buried in this beautiful doctrine of eternal families are rules about who can be sealed to each other.

For example, a widower could be sealed to their deceased spouse and, if they remarried, also be sealed to another woman. That meant if I married in the temple again, I would be sealed to Krista and whomever I married. Widows, however, can't be sealed to multiple men. If I married a widow, we could only be married "for time," which meant that our marriage wouldn't continue in the next life unless she canceled the sealing to her late husband. The only way we could be sealed to each other would be after our deaths when a living proxy could perform the sealing ordinance on our behalf. How the final family arrangements for men and women sealed to multiple spouses will work out in the next life is unknown. While the doctrine of eternal families is often discussed and preached from the pulpit and taught in classrooms at church, eternal polygamy, as it is sometimes called, is rarely, if ever, mentioned.

The irony of not wanting to date a widow wasn't lost on me. After all, I hoped my future dates would accept the fact that I was sealed to Krista. But how could I expect someone to accept my marriage to Krista when it was difficult for me to accept their sealing to someone else? Like with all the other widower-related questions, I had no answers. Until this evening, it was a topic I had thought little about and was too emotionally exhausted to dwell on any longer.

I powered down the computer and got ready for bed. Once under the covers, I couldn't fall asleep. The time spent online had reinforced the feelings of isolation and loneliness that permeated every aspect of my life. It made me realize that my widowed status might make dating difficult. I stared at the ceiling, wondering if marrying and having a family would ever happen or if I would spend the rest of this life alone.

CHAPTER THREE

Julianna

On a drive to see my boyfriend, Brian, I caught a glimpse of downtown Salt Lake City. Banners of ice skaters, skiers, and snowboarders draped the skyline and served as a backdrop to the 2002 Winter Olympics that were in full swing. But what caught my attention wasn't the skyscraper-sized banners, but the Salt Lake Temple. Its six gothic-themed granite spires were visible as I-15 curved to the south. The gold-leafed Angel Moroni statue atop the main spire sparkled with light from the setting sun and flickered like a yellow flame before disappearing behind one of the city's skyscrapers. Seeing the temple, the most famous and familiar symbol of The Church of Jesus Christ of Latter-day Saints, momentarily calmed the nervous feeling in my stomach.

The problem was that we lived on opposite ends of the Wasatch Front, the large metropolitan area of northern Utah. Brian lived in Provo, and I had recently moved to Ogden. That added up to eighty miles and a one-way drive of at least an hour and a half to see each other. Because of the distance, we saw each other only once, or sometimes twice, a week. Even though we talked on the phone most nights, the lack of in-person time made it feel like our three-month relationship had stalled.

I took partial responsibility for the distance between us. Two months earlier, just as we began dating, I moved to Ogden to be closer to work. I was employed by the Utah Department of Public Safety crime lab as a forensic scientist. I analyzed and identified drugs the police brought in from traffic stops and crime scenes. It was a fascinating job, and I enjoyed the work. The only thing I didn't like was the hour-long commute from my parents' home in Taylorsville, a suburb of Salt Lake City. I was excited to finally be on my own and take on the responsibilities that came with being an adult. The move was planned for months, but it just so happened that my mom set me up with Brian right before I signed a lease on an apartment in Ogden. We went out several times, and just as things started clicking, I moved.

I was hesitant to call Brian my "boyfriend." Even though he was the only person I was dating, we'd never discussed being exclusive, and lately it had seemed like neither of us were putting one hundred percent into the relationship. My biggest concern, however, was that Brian seemed okay with nightly phone calls and seeing each other once during the weekends. For me, phone calls only went so far. I believed if you were dating someone regularly, it was with the intent of moving the relationship forward—not something casual or convenient. I wanted to get married and start a family, and I didn't want to waste time with someone who didn't want the same thing.

Brian was a good guy. He checked most of the boxes I wanted in a future husband—he had a college education, a good job, wanted to get married in the temple, and have a family. He also attended church on Sundays and volunteered his time serving others in the congregation through various callings. However, I wasn't going to marry and spend eternity with someone who only matched up on paper and cross my fingers that things would work out. I wanted to be one-hundred-percent certain that the man I was dating would cherish me and make me the number-one person in his life.

It was dark and cold when I arrived at Brian's apartment, and I was tired and hungry. I was also nervous about the impending conversation, but I hoped that our evening together would result in a good discussion and a plan to see more of each other.

Brian's six-foot, two-hundred-pound frame took up most of the door when he opened it. He wore baggy jeans and a T-shirt. A baseball cap hid most of his red hair. He flashed me a broad smile and invited me inside.

"How was the drive?" he said after he gave me a quick squeeze.

"Long," I said. "There was still some rush-hour traffic."

"I'm glad you made it. I'm just finishing up some work. Give me a minute and we can get something to eat."

My stomach growled at the mention of food. Usually, I would have had dinner by now. Brian didn't say what he felt like eating, but with his healthy appetite, I knew the portions would be big and we wouldn't have to wait long for the food to arrive.

I followed Brian to his bedroom. Against one wall was a table with a desktop computer and a monitor. On the screen was the cover of a soon-to-be-published book. Brian worked as a videographer for a small start-up that turned books into visual stories. Video was his passion, and it seemed like he was always recording something with his camera or sitting at his computer editing footage. I sat on the edge of his bed and watched as he spliced some clips together.

"Where do you want to eat?" he said. "We haven't had Mexican in a while. How does that sound?"

There was a small hole-in-the-wall place a few miles from Brian's apartment that we frequented for the incredible burritos.

"Sure," I said. "That sounds great."

Brian finished up his work. Finally, he nodded his head in satisfaction then saved the file. A minute later we were in his car, heading to the restaurant.

On the way, we talked about our jobs. He told me more about the project he was working on. I told him about the large amount of cocaine the Utah Highway Patrol had brought in from a recent traffic stop. I considered broaching the subject of spending more time together, but decided to wait. There was no point in rushing it, especially when I was so tired and hungry. Waiting until I had some food would help me approach the situation better.

Thankfully, like I hoped, the restaurant wasn't very crowded, and we were seated immediately. Brian ordered street tacos and a soda. I got the supreme burrito and water. We both dug in to the chips and salsa on our table.

"How's marathon training going?" he asked between bites.

I had registered to run the Ogden Marathon in two months. It would be my second marathon, and I wanted to run it in under three and a half hours. Training was taking up a good portion of my free time.

"Really good," I said. "I'm hitting all of my pace and mileage goals."

"Are you running at your parents' house on Saturday?"

I nodded. Saturday training runs were anywhere between thirteen and twenty miles. I usually drove to my parents' home and ran there since my dad would drive the course and stop every three or four miles to give me water and words of encouragement.

"Do you want to get together after your run?" Brian said. "We could catch a movie or visit Temple Square."

His question caught me off guard. I hadn't expected to talk about weekend plans so soon. The butterflies in my stomach returned, fluttering wildly. It felt like they were going to fly out of my mouth. This seemed like a good opportunity to talk about spending more time together. I took a sip of water to give me a moment to gather my thoughts and to push the nervous feelings down.

"Let's go downtown," I said. "I haven't been to Temple Square in a while."

We worked out the details of our day, then I said, "Maybe we can make plans to see each other next week too."

Brian nodded in agreement. "Did you have something you wanted to do next Saturday?"

"Actually, I was thinking we could get together two or three nights after work next week."

My comment seemed to catch Brian by surprise. He was quiet for a minute then said, "Okay, we can get together during the week if you want. I think Wednesday should work."

"What about Monday, Wednesday, and Friday?"

Brian blinked. "How would we make *that* work?"

"I don't know. That's something we could figure out together. I just think we should see each other more than on the weekends."

Brian sipped his soda. "That's a lot of driving," he finally said.

"I know."

"Where would we meet? Your place? Mine?"

"I don't know for sure. That's what I want to figure out. We could meet halfway, like at my parents' place one night," I said, trying to recall the ideas I had brainstormed on the drive down.

"What's wrong with the schedule we have now?"

I tried to decipher the expression on his face. Was he serious or joking? Based on his knitted eyebrows and pursed lips, he was serious.

"I want to see you more often than that," I said.

"That's hard when you live in Ogden," he said. There was an edge to his words, as if reminding me it was my decision to move so far away.

The server stopped by our table and refilled our drinks. After she left, we ate in silence for several minutes. I picked at my burrito, my hunger replaced by frustration. While I didn't think we'd arrive at a solution that night, I had hoped we'd at least discuss some possibilities to think and pray about. I hadn't expected Brian to balk at the idea. Doubts about the relationship that had percolated in my mind on the drive to Provo resurfaced. Was it too soon to discuss this? Was I asking too much?

When the conversation started up again, we talked about the Winter Olympics that were wrapping up, the David Baldacci novel I was reading, and the movie *Blackhawk Down* that Brian and his roommates had seen two nights earlier. We didn't return to the topic of seeing each other more often until we got back to his apartment and I was getting ready to leave.

"We'll figure out a way to see each other more often," he said after giving me a goodbye hug.

"I know we will," I said, even though inside I wasn't so sure.

On the drive home, I was too tired to think of other solutions, so I turned on the radio to keep me awake. As the lights of Ogden came into view, I wondered if I'd made the right choice to relocate. Before leasing the apartment, I had prayed about my decision and felt it was the right thing to do. But that night, I found myself second-guessing the move.

It was after eleven when I arrived home. I was exhausted and not looking forward to getting up at five a.m. for my eight-mile training run. I quickly got ready for bed. I was tempted just to dive under the covers and go to sleep, but I managed to find the strength to get on my knees, say a quick prayer, and ask God for reassurance that moving to Ogden had been the right thing to do.

CHAPTER FOUR
Abel

My date was a woman named Stephanie. She was an artist and made a living creating western-themed bronze sculptures of cowboys and horses. In lieu of a headshot, she posted photographs of her work, so this was the first time I'd actually seen her. Stephanie was in her late twenties with moss-green eyes. Her auburn hair was pulled back in a ponytail that fell between her shoulder blades. She had a smattering of freckles on her cheeks. She was the fourth woman I had gone out with, and the first one where I felt that I wasn't cheating on Krista.

My first date a few weeks earlier was awful. Overwhelmed by feelings of guilt and infidelity, it was difficult to carry on a basic conversation. In addition, I spent the entire time looking over my shoulder, worried someone I knew would see me and tell Krista about my secret rendezvous. My second and third dates, each with a different woman, went better, though I still felt like I was stepping out on my late wife. This time, however, in a Mexican restaurant with bowls of tortilla chips and dark-red salsa between us, I didn't feel guilty. I didn't know if this was a natural evolution that came with dating or if there was something about Stephanie's quiet personality that put me at ease. Whatever the reason, it was nice to enjoy a meal with an attractive woman without feeling like I was doing something wrong.

Still, I wasn't completely comfortable. The restaurant was popular and located just two miles from my home. The odds of running into someone I knew on a Saturday afternoon were high. When we entered, I had scanned the restaurant for familiar faces, but didn't recognize anyone. My friends and family didn't know about my dating, and I was unsure how I'd introduce Stephanie if we ran into one of them. A friend? Acquaintance? Certainly not a date.

At this moment, my biggest challenge was to keep the conversation going. It turned out that Stephanie was extremely shy, and getting her to say more than a sentence or two at a time was a challenge. I had plenty to say, but everything I wanted to share revolved around my life and marriage to Krista. I couldn't explain this urge to tell stories about her, and I didn't know if it was normal. Hours of online research on this topic had left me with more questions than answers. On previous dates, I let the women take the lead when discussing Krista and our marriage. I'd answer their questions, but wouldn't voluntarily divulge any other information. I worried that talking too much about Krista would leave me in tears or make my dates think I wasn't ready for a relationship.

So far, all the Krista-related questions had been surface level. "How long were you married?" "When did your wife die?" "How did she pass away?" "Do you have any children?" Telling them Krista died five months ago, and she was seven months pregnant when she took her own life, was enough to stop them from probing deeper. I was glad the conversations stopped there. I didn't know how I'd handle discussing hearing the gunshot that killed Krista or taking my daughter, Hope, off life support nine days later. Crying on a first date didn't seem like the best way to get a second one.

Instead, I let my dates talk about themselves. I asked about their family, hobbies, their jobs, where they were from, and places they'd traveled. Those topics were usually more than enough to keep them talking. Except with Stephanie. When I asked her questions, she responded in one- or two-word sentences.

"What's the most interesting place you've visited?" I said, using one of my tried-and-true questions.

"England."

"Where in England?"

"London."

"What did you like most about London?"

"Buckingham Palace."

It wasn't until I asked about her art that her face brightened and she described, in detail, the work and effort it took to create life-size bronze sculptures.

By the time our food arrived—two enchiladas for her, chicken mole for me—it was Stephanie's turn to ask questions. Instead of asking what I did for a living, hobbies, or what I liked to do for fun like my previous dates had done, Stephanie said, "So, you're a widower."

I tensed, not expecting the topic to come up so soon. On past dates, it was a subject women eased into the same way one lowered themselves into an ice bath. Caught unprepared, I wasn't sure how much to say or what she wanted to know.

"That's right," I replied.

I waited for a follow-up question, but one didn't come. To break the silence, I added, "We were married almost three years."

I tried reading Stephanie's expression, but her face remained neutral.

Finally, she asked, "Do you have any kids?"

"None living. My wife was pregnant when she died."

Stephanie's eyes widened while a lump formed in my throat. A familiar but uncomfortable silence settled over the table. I wasn't sure if the silence was because she didn't know what else to say or because she was shy. Memories of Hope's short life flashed through my mind—seeing her for the first time in the newborn intensive care unit, holding her as she took her last breath, carrying her casket to her final resting place. Tears welled up in the corners of my eyes and I knew if I didn't get my emotions under control, the evening was going to turn even more awkward for both of us.

"I removed my daughter from life support nine days after my wife died. Sorry to spring it on you like that, but I haven't figured out how to put that into my dating profile."

"I'm sorry," Stephanie said. "It must have been hard to lose two people you love."

"It was, but I'm doing my best to move forward," I said as I blinked back tears.

Another pause. "How long ago did your wife die?"

"November," I said. This sounded better than saying "five months." While Stephanie did the math in her head, I tried to come up with a plausible explanation for why I was dating so soon just in case she asked. Even though I'd had months to figure out an answer, I still didn't know what to say.

Stephanie raised her left eyebrow. I couldn't tell whether she was pondering her next question or deciding if she should run screaming from the restaurant.

She went with the question.

"Were you and your wife married in the temple?"

"Yes. The one in Logan," I said.

I was grateful we were no longer talking about Hope. My tears in retreat, I watched Stephanie's reaction carefully, knowing that this could be a dealbreaker. While getting to know some of my online matches better, a few had said they didn't want to pursue a relationship once they learned Krista and I were sealed. "I don't want to be wife number two" or "I'm not doing the eternal polygamy thing" were the most common responses. Though their comments stung, I was learning not to take those remarks personally. If they didn't want to date a widower, it was something I'd rather know upfront than after our relationship became serious and I had feelings for them. I made a mental note to update my online dating profile, hoping that would help avoid these awkward moments in the future.

Stephanie nodded and looked down at her plate. Though she didn't say what she was thinking, she didn't have to. I let the silence hang and took a bite of my food. Finally, I jump-started the conversation, steering it away from Krista.

"Do you have a favorite sculpture you created?"

Stephanie's face lightened up at the question, and she told me about a commissioned work she had completed last year. I kept the conversation going through the rest of our meal. At some point, she asked questions about my job and my two-year Latter-day Saint mission to Bulgaria, but the subject never returned to Krista.

After our meal, I drove her back to my place where she had parked her truck. Neither of us brought up the possibility of getting together again. I was okay with that. I'd had dinner with an attractive woman without feeling guilty. It was a minor victory, but an important one. The issue for the future was no longer whether I could date, but finding someone who could accept my marital status both in this world and the next one, along with all the unknowns. The way things were going, I wondered if I'd be playing this dating game for a long, long time.

CHAPTER FIVE

Julianna

    I lay stomach-down on my parents' trampoline to recover from my fourteen-mile run and soak up some warm April sunshine. In one hand, I held the latest Lee Child novel, and in the other, a twelve-ounce bottle of chocolate milk—my reward for successfully completing another week of training. I put the book to the side, closed my eyes, and enjoyed the sun's heat on my legs and back.

    The run was great. I felt good the entire time and finished five minutes faster than my goal. Though the Ogden Marathon was still a month away, today had given me hope that I could complete the race in about three hours. However, the faster-than-anticipated pace left me exhausted. I should have been cleaning up and getting ready for my date with Brian, but all I wanted to do was take a nap.

    After a few minutes, I turned onto my back and reached for my cell phone, a bronze-colored Nokia that had slid to the center of the trampoline. It surprised me that Brian hadn't called. Most Saturdays, there was a voicemail waiting when I finished running. Today there were no missed calls. I dialed his number and focused on the wispy cirrus clouds that reminded me of strands of tangled hair.

Brian picked up on the fourth ring.

"Hey, Julie," he said. His voice sounded tired.

"Did I wake you up?" I said, glancing at my watch. It was ten thirty.

"Sort of. Played video games with the roommates until late last night."

"Sounds like fun. When can I expect to see you?"

"What time is it?" he said.

There was a muffled sound, followed by a grunt. I pictured Brian turning over to look at the red numbers of the alarm clock he kept next to his bed.

"Do you still want to go downtown?" he said. The words came out like a groan, and I felt my heart drop as I realized the plans we had made to visit Temple Square, get something to eat, and perhaps some shopping weren't going to happen.

"I just want to spend the day with you," I said. "I don't care what we do."

"Why don't you come to my place instead? We can hike Bridal Veil Falls."

Bridal Veil Falls was a short, popular trail up Provo Canyon that led to a waterfall. With the spring runoff, the falls were bound to be quite the sight. I liked the activity, but didn't like the thought of driving all the way to Provo. My legs and back ached, and I didn't know how they'd handle sitting in the car for a forty-five-minute drive to Provo.

"I thought we were meeting at my parents' house," I said.

"I need to shower and get dressed," he replied.

"I still need to clean up from my run."

"Take your time. I'll be ready when you arrive."

I sighed, perhaps too loudly.

"If it makes you feel better, I'll drive to Ogden the next week or two," he said. I'm just really tired this morning."

I am too, I thought, but stopped myself from verbalizing it.

"If you're too tired to hike, we can catch a movie," Brian said. "We can get a bite to eat before the show."

"Fine," I said, trying not to let my frustration escape. "I'll call you when I'm on my way."

"Perfect," he said.

"See you soon," I replied.

I grabbed my paperback, drank the rest of my chocolate milk, and eased myself off the trampoline. My exasperation grew with each step I took. I was mad for giving in so easily and wished I had pressed Brian harder to drive here. After our talk in February, we had worked out a plan to see each other more often but it never happened. Lately, it was feeling like I was the one making all the sacrifices to spend time together.

Near the back door, my dad was on his hands and knees replacing a sprinkler head. His T-shirt, stretched tight over his fit body, was peppered with mud.

"Is Brian stopping by?" he asked as I slid the patio door open.

"No."

"Why not?"

"He's too tired to make the drive."

"That's too bad. I was looking forward to catching up with him."

I stepped inside, stopped, then turned back. When it came to relationship advice, Dad was my go-to person. He had a rational way of approaching issues that clicked with my logical, scientific mind. He also helped me better understand men by explaining the motivations behind their words and actions.

"When you and Mom were dating, was it hard to find time for each other?" I knew the story of how they met at a dance class, but I couldn't remember either of them mentioning not spending time together. Perhaps there was more to their story.

My dad thought for a moment. "Not that I recall."

"It probably helped that you lived close to each other."

"Yes, but we were both busy with school, jobs, and church callings. We made it work, though."

I mulled over my dad's words and reflected on how hard it was to spend time with Brian. I wondered how my parents would have navigated the challenges of a long-distance relationship. Probably better than Brian and I were handling things.

My dad had taught me to set high standards for the men I dated and not to settle for someone who couldn't meet my expectations. It was important to me to spend as much time as possible with whoever I dated since we might be together for eternity. Lately, I'd wondered how invested Brian was in our relationship, but I also felt some guilt over my move to Ogden.

"Everything all right, Julie?"

My dad's words brought me out of my thoughts. Should I mention my worries to him? I decided to see how the afternoon went instead.

"Everything's fine," I said. I headed inside to clean up and prepare myself for the drive to Provo.

CHAPTER SIX

Abel

The morning after my date with Stephanie, I checked the LDSsingles site for new matches. I had dated or reached out to all of my other "top matches" and hoped to find someone new to connect with.

There was one new woman.

I looked at her headshot and read her profile. Though she came across as creative, smart, accomplished, and witty—all things I wanted in a future spouse—there was no physical attraction. Rejecting someone solely because of their looks made me feel shallow. What if I was bypassing a potential soulmate?

There was, of course, more to a relationship than physical appearance. A year before Krista and I became a couple, I dated an attractive coed I met at our work-study job. She was beautiful, but we never connected on a mental, emotional, or spiritual level. The relationship only lasted five months. Krista, however, was gorgeous inside and out.

What first attracted me to Krista was her yellow hair, ice-blue eyes, and curves in the right places and in the right proportions. There was a deeper connection too, but that came after getting to know her better. What moved our relationship from dating to marriage was the perfect blend of physical attraction, shared interests, emotional connections, and a spiritual bond. I don't believe we would have tied the knot if one of those pieces was missing. Knowing the effort it took to make a marriage work, it didn't seem right to settle for someone who didn't meet all my criteria, and I didn't want whomever I married to feel like they had settled either. I wanted to check all of their boxes too.

With no other matches to contact, I considered expanding my search, but I was unsure what to change. Age range? Physical characteristics? Interests? I knew exactly what I was looking for. Why alter a formula that worked?

But was it really working?

The four women I'd gone out with were everything I wanted—on paper. They were attractive, creative, smart, outgoing, and supposedly active members of the same faith. We had great rapport in emails and messages. But when we met in person, the connection I sought was missing. I thought there'd be a spark with one of them. Instead, there was nothing. Was this because I was still in love with Krista, or that grief and guilt had clouded my judgment? The axiom that widowed folks should wait at least a year before dating flashed through my mind. I still didn't know the reason for that supposed rule, but perhaps it had something to do with giving the heart time to heal. Maybe I was dating too soon and needed more time before I could connect on more than a physical level.

If it was simply a matter of waiting, I could do that. What worried me, however, was that finding deep love—the kind where you bonded with another soul—comes around only once in a lifetime. If that was the case, I was in trouble. The desire for a relationship, to marry and start a family again, was so strong that I could see myself doing it with someone I didn't fully love. But I didn't want companionship. I wanted a relationship with a woman for whom I would swim oceans, climb mountains, and slay dragons to prove my love.

Someone like Krista.

I had never believed in soulmates or that there was only one person I could fall in love with. I thought there were many women I could happily spend the rest of my life with. The challenge was finding one of them. Krista was one. Could I find someone else? I replayed my four recent dates over in my mind. Each woman had part, but not all, of what I was looking for. I thought back to my date with Stephanie. She was attractive, and we shared an interest in art and creative endeavors, but I didn't mesh with her shy personality. I didn't need someone as gregarious or outgoing as Krista, but I wanted someone who could express herself in more than one-word sentences. Perhaps Stephanie would have opened up more on a second or third date. That question, at least with Stephanie, would go unanswered. But maybe something would happen if I gave my next date a second chance. Maybe a little patience was all it took to feel that spark.

A knock on my door brought me out of my thoughts. I wasn't expecting anyone and wondered who it would be. I turned off the computer and went to investigate. The smell of warm bread engulfed me as I opened the door. My mom held a loaf of homemade bread in her hands. My stomach growled in anticipation. My mom makes delicious bread.

"Just came by to see how you're doing," she said.

"Thank you," I said, taking the warm loaf from her hands. "It smells wonderful. I'll have some for breakfast."

"Who was at your place yesterday?" my mom asked.

The question caught me off guard.

"What?"

"Yesterday, I saw a woman stop by. Who was she?"

It took a moment for it to click. Stephanie. My mom had seen Stephanie. We had met at my place before driving to the restaurant. After our date, she had spent a few minutes inside my house before leaving. My mom probably glanced out the window, saw Stephanie coming or going, or noticed a strange truck parked in front of my home and kept an eye out until we returned. So much for keeping my dating life a secret.

I didn't think my mom was spying. I lived on the same street as my parents. Some would say I lived next door, but that wasn't completely accurate. There was an acre and a half of fallow land that separated our homes. The distance provided some privacy, but obviously not enough. Though I knew someone might see Stephanie when she stopped at my place, I thought the risk was small and acceptable. I was wrong. Had Mom brought the bread over as an excuse to talk to me about my date?

I considered telling my mom that Stephanie was just an old friend, but hiding my dating life couldn't go on forever, so I told her the truth.

"She was someone I went out with," I said, trying to keep my tone as nonchalant as possible.

"What do you mean, you went out with her? Like, a date?"

"Yeah."

"Abel, are you dating?"

Her words were a mix of astonishment, surprise, and horror.

"Yeah," I said.

"How long has this been going on?"

"A while," I said.

I didn't want to go into further detail, and thankfully, my mom didn't push the issue, but the shocked look on her face told me there would be a future conversation about it. Before closing the door, I watched her slowly walk home. I put the bread on the counter to eat later. My appetite was gone.

My mom's stunned reaction was the main reason I had kept my dating activities secret. How does one tell those who are still grieving their sister, granddaughter, friend, and daughter-in-law that you're going out with someone else? It still wasn't something I could explain. While I didn't expect my mom to understand my actions, I certainly didn't need her, or anyone else, poking around in my private life or second-guessing my decisions while I figured things out. I made a note not to bring any dates back to my place for a while. The last thing I wanted was for my mom or others to drop by with bread or some other treat whenever they noticed a strange car in the driveway.

•••

To avoid another conversation about my personal life, instead of sitting with my family at church, I moved to the back pew, where the few unmarried and divorced men congregated. I tried to focus on the service, but my mind kept returning to dating, my mom's reaction, and whether I could ever love someone as much as Krista. Consumed by this train of thought, the meeting passed quickly. The next thing I knew, the din of conversation filled the chapel and families filed by on their way to Sunday School and other classes.

Waiting for the chapel to clear, I noticed a woman walking up the far aisle. She was tall, with curly strands of corn-silk colored hair that hung past her shoulders. She had a lean, athletic build, and the tan skin of someone who spent a lot of time in the sun. I found her drop-dead gorgeous and couldn't take my eyes off her. I knew most everyone in the congregation, but I hadn't seen this woman before. Was she a visitor, or a recent move-in? A new apartment complex had opened about a half mile from the church and had brought with it a steady stream of people, mostly young married couples, to services on Sunday. I wondered if she lived there, and more importantly, if she was married.

Then something strange happened.

As she drew closer, what I can only describe as a surge of energy filled my body. It was warm and soothing, yet powerful enough that every hair on my body felt like it was standing on end. With each step she took, the electric feeling grew in intensity. It reached its apex as she passed, then faded as she walked out the chapel doors toward Sunday School.

I stared at the empty doorway. I'd never experienced a sensation like that before. It was more than mere physical attraction. It was as if this beautiful mystery woman radiated energy.

Who was she?

I had to find out.

I threw a quick glance over my shoulder to make sure my mom wasn't looking, then went in search of this woman.

CHAPTER SEVEN

Julianna

I never mastered the art of flirting. In high school, I thought if I smiled at a guy, he'd know I wanted to get to know him better. By the time I learned boys didn't equate smiling with flirting, I had already graduated from high school. I adjusted my technique in college but I was still unsuccessful at attracting the attention of my male peers. Better flirting techniques helped a little, but I was extremely shy. I struggled to maintain eye contact and engage in small talk. During parties, study groups, and other activities, I preferred to observe and listen instead of engaging. If male students approached me, it was because they needed a tutor to help them with their chemistry or math assignments.

So naturally, I rarely dated—maybe once every six or eight weeks. I went out with a handful of guys more than once, but never felt a connection or wanted the relationship to become serious. I wanted to be outgoing and date more often, but I could never fully emerge from my shell. By the time I graduated, I still hadn't experienced a serious relationship.

Like most Latter-day Saint women, I dreamed of finding a husband and getting sealed in the temple—something I was certain would happen during college. After all, that's when my parents and extended family members had met their matches. To add to the pressure, most of my high school and neighborhood friends had tied the knot, gotten engaged, or were involved in a serious relationship during their college years. When I received my diploma at twenty-two, my love life was nonexistent. The pressure to marry was cultural, not something I felt from family or close friends. There was still plenty of time to find a husband and start a family. Still, when my sister Dede, eighteen months younger, got engaged and married her first year of college, I was jealous.

Then I met Brian, my first serious relationship. We didn't get together because I figured out flirting or because he noticed me at a party. Instead, my mom and a mutual friend set us up. Things went well enough that our first date turned into a second and the second into a third. As our relationship was starting, I moved to Ogden, and it never really progressed and it wasn't getting better. In the weeks following our talk at the Mexican restaurant, the progress I hoped for wasn't happening.

Today, after my fifteen-mile training run, Brian drove to Ogden and we had spent the day together. We drove to several stores looking for, and eventually finding, a new pair of running shoes. I gave him a tour of the crime lab where I worked, and then we shared some orange chicken and beef and broccoli at a local Chinese restaurant. We wrapped up the day by renting a movie. I had enjoyed every moment. This was the kind of time I wanted to spend with him as often as possible. As we watched the movie, I hoped he had enjoyed the day as much as I had. Maybe when the movie ended we could have another talk about having days like this more often.

As the credits rolled, Brian stood and yawned.

"Can you stay awake driving home?" I asked.

"I'll probably crash at my parents' house," he said.

Brian's parents lived in Layton, a suburb fifteen miles south of Ogden. Staying at my place wasn't an option. In the Latter-day Saint faith, premarital sex is forbidden. Even sleeping under the same roof could trigger rumors or put us into a precarious situation.

As he was tying his shoes, I had an idea on how we could spend the day together. "Why don't you come to church with me tomorrow?"

"I didn't bring any Sunday clothes," he replied.

Latter-day Saint men typically wear white shirts and ties to church. Brian was wearing navy cargo shorts and a polo shirt. Occasionally, I had seen people come to church in similar attire. His clothing might raise a few eyebrows and some might think I had brought a non-member investigator to the service, but it wouldn't go further than that.

I wanted to kick myself for not thinking about inviting him to church before our date. With a little planning, we could have easily spent most of Sunday together. I made a mental note to bring this up next time he came to Ogden, then voiced a few alternatives.

"Maybe your dad or one of your bothers has a shirt and tie you can borrow," I said.

Brian gave me a half smile and said, "Next time."

"Come as you are. No one will care."

"I know," he said, "but I'd still feel out of place."

Suddenly, I realized that despite dating for four months, we'd never attended church together. In the Latter-day Saint culture, going to church with the person you're dating is important, and we had yet to do it. My faith was central to my life and I wanted to share that experience with the person I was dating. It stung that Brian turned down my offer.

Brian must have noticed an expression of pain on my face. "What's wrong?" he asked.

"I want to spend more time with you," I said.

"I'll go to church with you next time I'm in Ogden," he said.

I considered making one last plea, but I decided not to push it. I had enjoyed our time together and didn't want to end things on a sour note. I gave Brian a hug as he headed out the door.

•••

The next morning, I awoke from hunger pangs, but I wasn't ready to get out of bed. Sunday was the only day of the week I could sleep in. It was a day to rest, relax, and recharge, a chance to prepare myself mentally, physically, and spiritually for the coming week. I wanted to sleep for another hour or two. I turned on my side and closed my eyes, but my hunger wouldn't abate. I got up and made breakfast—two eggs over hard, two pieces of toast, and some cereal. Then I went back to bed, hoping my full stomach would make me tired, but by this point I was wide awake. I gave up my attempts at sleep and started getting ready for the day.

I was curling my hair when my dad called. I put him on speaker. "You hurried home after the run yesterday," he said after we exchanged pleasantries. "I wanted to check in and see how things went with Brian." Some people might find my dad's call intrusive, but my dad was a good sounding board for relationships. He knows how guys think, and I trust his opinion and insights. I summed up my date with Brian for him.

"I'm glad you spent the day together," he said. "It's been a while since that happened."

"I wish we were spending today together," I said, curling another strand of hair.

"What do you mean, Julie?"

As I ran more hair through the curling iron, I told my dad about our conversation and Brian's decision not to come to church.

"Am I making a big deal out of nothing?" I asked.

"I don't think so. Attending church and spending time with Brian are important to you. It's okay to be disappointed."

My dad's words came as a relief. My lack of relationship experience made me second-guess myself, and I sometimes wondered if I expected too much from the guys I dated.

"You can't control what choices Brian makes," my dad continued. "Let him make his own decisions. But you can infer what's important to him by the actions he does or doesn't take. People typically express their true feelings through their actions—not their words."

I set the curling iron on the counter by the sink and replayed yesterday in my mind. Yes, Brian had driven to Ogden and we had spent most of the day together, but he also turned down a chance to spend more time with me. I understood what my dad was saying, though I didn't want to admit to myself what it meant.

When I left for church an hour later, my dad's thoughts weighed heavily on my mind. I paused inside the chapel doors and looked for a place to sit. The chapel was mostly full, and everyone was sitting with a spouse, children, or friends. Even the gray-haired widows who sat on the opposite side of the chapel were sitting with someone. I spotted an empty pew near the front and sat there.

The service began, and I tried to focus on the music, the prayers, and the spiritual messages—anything to distract myself from the fact that I was sitting alone. Normally, that wouldn't bother me, but today I knew the reason I had a pew to myself was because Brian had chosen to attend another ward.

CHAPTER EIGHT

Abel

Each Sunday for the next month, I collected pieces of information about the mystery woman. The first thing I learned was her name: Julianna Taylor. Once I had that information, the ward directory gave me her address and phone number. My assumption that she lived in the new apartment complex was correct. From a chance conversation with a ward member who was also a police officer, I learned that Julianna worked as a forensic analyst in the nearby state crime lab.

It felt like I was putting together a puzzle without a picture. I didn't know what the final image looked like, but each time I connected two pieces, they made an incomplete but alluring portrait. However, learning about her in bits was a slow and tedious process. I could only connect a few pieces each Sunday and needed hundreds of pieces more. I finally decided that talking to her directly would fill in the blanks a lot faster.

What I couldn't figure out was whether Julianna was in a serious relationship. The fact that she didn't wear a wedding ring and attended church alone indicated she wasn't, but I knew better than to assume. After being widowed, I hadn't removed my wedding band. This led to a handful of awkward conversations with salespeople and strangers who thought I was married. Maybe she was divorced or dating someone who didn't attend church. Maybe she had a husband and a good reason for not wearing a wedding ring.

If I belonged to any other ward, I would have already introduced myself. However, Krista and I had grown up in this ward, and most of the congregation were neighbors and friends we had known most of our lives. Many of them were our Sunday School teachers or youth leaders. Our engagement thrilled the entire congregation, and most had attended our wedding or reception. Krista's suicide had sent shock waves through our tight-knit community. Many were still grieving her death. In addition, my parents, three younger siblings, Krista's grandmother, Loretta, her brother, Scott, and Krista's best friend, Beckah, all attended the same church. How would they react if I dated Julianna? Would church become unbearable? It was only in the last month that I could attend church without shouldering the weight of the congregations' stares and unanswered questions. A relationship with Julianna would thrust me back into the spotlight. The last thing I wanted was attention.

I knew watching her from a distance wouldn't accomplish anything. A woman that beautiful wouldn't be single for long, especially in a faith that prioritizes marriage and families. The odds of her starting a conversation with me were slim. If I was serious about dating her, I needed to overcome my worries and endure any resulting fallout. However, every time I thought about approaching her, fear of how others might react stopped me from acting.

One Sunday, about a month after I first noticed Julianna, everything changed. The day started out like normal. I woke up wondering if she would be at church. When I arrived just as the services started, I saw her sitting in her usual pew near the front. I settled back into my normal seat near the back and imagined approaching her and striking up a conversation. My fantasy abruptly ended a few minutes later when the services began and the bishop made a surprise announcement—the boundaries of the ward were changing.

In the Latter-day Saint faith, instead of attending the church closest to you or picking a congregation or a bishop, each ward has geographic boundaries. Members who live within those boundaries attend their assigned congregation. In Utah, where most people are Latter-day Saints, ward boundaries can be as small as two or three close neighborhoods. In states and countries where fewer members of the Church live, boundaries are as large as cities or counties. As the population of members within the area grows or shrinks, ward boundaries are periodically redrawn. Sometimes the adjustments are minor. Other times, brand-new wards are created and others discontinued.

Even though the bishop's announcement stunned me, it didn't come as a complete surprise. The new apartment complex where Julianna lived had doubled the size of the congregation. Every week, there were new faces in attendance, and seating was often at a premium. In the past, I had greeted boundary adjustments with a mix of curiosity and anticipation, but I never had a personal stake in them. I always found these changes to be positive as they brought in new people with fresh energy and ideas. In our case, shrinking the boundaries made it easier to know everyone better and make Sunday worship a more intimate experience.

Not everyone took such a blasé approach. I recalled past boundary changes that left fellow ward members in tears because their friends would meet at different times or in different buildings. After today's announcement, I now understood exactly how they felt. Because Julianna and I lived on opposite corners of the ward, we'd probably end up attending different services starting next Sunday. Attending different congregations was like living in different worlds, so if I wanted to reach out to her, the getting-to-know-you conversation had to be today.

I decided the best time was right after church when people were rounding up their families and were too busy to pay much attention if they spotted us talking. In Sunday School, I sat in the seat behind Julianna and listened as other ward members speculated about the new boundaries. One person wondered if they would divide the apartment complex between other wards. Another said the apartments would be assigned to a different congregation. A third talked about splitting up our ward in three or four pieces. Instead of giving me hope, each rumor reinforced the notion that Julianna and I would find ourselves attending different services next week. I tried to convince myself that this would be a good thing because if we dated, those who knew me and Krista couldn't scrutinize my new relationship, but I knew the odds of connecting with Julianna next Sunday were slim.

After Sunday School, I headed to priesthood meeting, determined to make contact right after church. When the meeting ended, I hurried through the packed hallways looking for Julianna, but couldn't find her. With a heavy feeling in my stomach, I made my way to the parking lot, hoping to see her bronze-colored Saturn but she'd already left. My shoulders sagged in disappointment, and I wondered if I'd ever see her again.

At home, I tried to console myself by looking for new matches on LDSsingles. There were a few new women, but my thoughts were so consumed with Julianna, I couldn't concentrate long enough to message them. Instead, I recalled all the missed opportunities to talk with Julianna in person. I had let my own fears and the thoughts, cares, and feelings of other people dictate my actions. As a result, I'd never know if the connection I felt toward her was real or imaginary. Right then, I vowed never to let the thoughts and concerns of others influence my decisions again.

•••

That evening, as time for the meeting to announce the new ward boundaries approached, I considered not attending. There was something about seeing Julianna's residence split off from the rest of the ward that felt like pouring the proverbial salt into an open wound. Besides, my mom would be there and would fill me in on the details later. At the last minute, however, I got in my car and drove to the church. I had to know which ward Julianna ended up in. That was the one thing my mom wouldn't know to tell me.

The chapel and overflow area were packed by the time I arrived. My mom had saved me a seat and waved me over. Krista's grandmother sat two rows in front of us next to the same group of widowed neighbors she sat with during worship services. As I took my seat next to my mom, I glanced over my shoulder at the packed overflow area. Julianna sat by herself near the back. For some reason, it had never occurred to me she'd attend. Nervous excitement coursed through my body as I realized this meeting gave us a final chance to talk.

Boundary change meetings were usually short and to the point, but this one dragged on forever. A prayer. A hymn. A talk about inspired changes. All seemed to take longer than normal. To help pass the time, I glanced back at Julianna and thought about the best way to strike up a conversation. Finally, the new boundaries were unveiled. What I saw shocked me. The boundaries of our ward had only two changes. The biggest adjustment was the apartment complex. They assigned each apartment building to a different ward. Building E, the one Julianna lived in, was assigned to our congregation.

I did a double take. This couldn't be real, could it? I looked again. Julianna and I were still in the same ward. A baffled excitement replaced all my anxiety and worry. If there was a heavenly sign about these boundary changes, this was it.

I looked back at Julianna. She appeared to be studying the new boundaries. She took a pen from her purse and wrote something on a piece of paper. The electric sensation I had felt a few weeks earlier returned, but this time accompanied by the thought that I needed to ask her out. I was considering talking with her after the meeting when my mom nudged me with her elbow.

"Loretta's not in the ward anymore," she said.

At first, I didn't understand who my mom was referring to, and it took a moment before I realized she was talking about Krista's grandmother. I turned my attention back to the screen. The only other alteration to the ward's boundaries affected Loretta. Her neighborhood was now part of an adjoining ward. I glanced over at Loretta, who was sitting with several of her neighbors. The way their white and gray-haired heads bobbed from the screen back to each other made it look like they were discussing the changes.

I didn't know how to feel about this development. Loretta had practically raised Krista and her brother Scott. Krista had lovingly referred to Loretta as her "proper English grandmother," and I always believed it was because of Loretta's guidance and influence that Krista turned out to be the remarkable, amazing woman I fell in love with. I considered Loretta, instead of Krista's birth mother, as my actual mother-in-law. I talked to her at church and stopped by her place several times a month to see how she was doing. Church wouldn't feel the same without her in the pews. However, having Loretta attend a different ward would make a relationship with Julianna easier—assuming things went that far. In some ways, it would be a sweet mercy for her not to see me with Julianna every Sunday.

After a few more words about the changes, the meeting ended. As the chapel filled with the white noise of conversation, I glanced back at Julianna, who hurried toward the exit. The electric feeling returned. I considered catching up with her and using the new ward boundaries as an excuse to start a conversation, but decided it could wait until next Sunday.

As she exited the building, the afternoon sunlight caught her hair and a bright yellow glow enveloped her. The door closed, and both Julianna and the warm, electric feeling vanished.

CHAPTER NINE

Julianna

The morning of the Ogden Marathon, I awoke at 3:59 a.m., one minute before my alarm rang. I lay in bed and stared into the dark until the clock beeped. I dressed in purple shorts and a white singlet, ate some cereal and a banana, and was out the door by 4:30. The air felt crisp and cold—perfect weather for a twenty-six-point-two-mile race.

With barely any traffic, it only took ten minutes to reach downtown Ogden. Soon I was on a bus packed with a hundred other runners heading toward South Fork, a mountain valley twenty miles east. I settled into my seat, closed my eyes, and mentally prepared myself for the run. I had two goals for the race. The first was to qualify for the Boston Marathon, which meant finishing the race in under three hours and forty minutes. Barring a serious race-related injury, I wasn't worried about achieving that goal. My training led me to believe I could finish in about three hours and fifteen minutes. However, I wanted to push myself and see if I could achieve my second goal: completing the race in three hours.

The bus dropped us off on a narrow two-lane road. Aside from the floodlights that illuminated the starting area, it was pitch black. It was colder in the mountains than in Ogden, and goose bumps spread along my arms and legs. Most runners huddled in small groups to talk and keep warm, but I moved toward the starting line. In my first marathon, I waited until the last minute to move forward, and I ended up in the middle of the pack. As a result, it took several minutes to cross the starting line and another mile to weave through the crowd and hit my stride. I wouldn't make that mistake again.

Gradually, the morning light revealed pastures, distant trees, and a road that went straight for a half mile before curving amidst rolling hills. As the sun crested the horizon, we were told to approach the starting line. The clusters of people dissolved and pushed their way forward, forming into one large mass. Runners of all ages and genders tried to elbow their way in front of me, but I held my ground.

A minute later, the race began.

For the first three miles, I stayed with a group of fifteen runners. As the miles passed, they slowed and dropped back one by one. By the time we came out of the canyon, five miles later, it was me and another runner—a man in his late thirties who wore a matching dark blue singlet and running shorts and had thick, black hair on his arms. As we ran, we chatted about past marathons we had run. He did most of the talking as he had a solid decade of running behind him. This was my second marathon so I didn't have as much to say. Still, it was nice to have some company as it helped pass the time and the miles.

As we followed the road along the north side of Pineview Reservoir a female spectator took a step into the road and yelled at me, "You're in third place!"

Her comment surprised me. Was I really in third place? I had been concentrating on keeping my pace and I hadn't been paying attention to how many female runners I had passed.

My running companion chuckled and said, "The last time I ran a marathon, I ran for several miles with the woman who ended up winning it. Maybe you'll do the same."

"That's not going to happen," I said shaking my head.

We continued chatting until the road turned into a hill and the man's place slowed.

"Run fast and win the race!" he said as I pulled ahead.

"I'll try," I said even though I wasn't expecting to see the other two runners.

Around the next curve, I saw the second-place female runner. The hills had slowed her pace and I set my sights on her. A quarter mile later, I passed her. Though I could see some male runners ahead of me, I couldn't see the lead female runner. I pushed thoughts of winning from my mind and focused on hitting my goal of a three-hour finish.

At mile eighteen, I ran across the top of Pineview Dam. By this point in the race, I was alone. This wasn't good. Unless I was winning, I wanted to see other runners as they gave me something to focus on, as well as the motivation to run faster and pass them. Running alone made it easier to relax, slow down, and lose focus. I increased my pace, hoping to see someone soon.

Just then a spectator wearing a purple Utah Jazz T-shirt stepped out on the road and cupped his hands to his mouth.

"If you push it, you can catch the leader!" he yelled. "She's not doing great. I watched her throw up."

I wiped the sweat from my eyes. We were in a canyon and with the curvature of the road, I couldn't see more than a third of a mile. Maybe the leader was around the turn, barely out of sight. It was impossible to know whether the man was right, but his words gave me the mental strength to keep my pace and not slow down.

I didn't see the lead female running around the next curve or the one after that. It wasn't until the twenty-third mile as the course exited Ogden Canyon that she came into view. She was running at a good clip but from the way her body was hunched, it looked like she was in pain. I focused my attention on her and increased my pace. A quarter mile later, I pulled even. Our eyes met for a fraction of a second and a surprised look flashed across her face. Before she could recover, I gave it one last push, and she disappeared from my peripheral vision. I kept running and didn't look back.

The course wound its way along the Ogden River, along parks and green space until it came out on Washington Boulevard. The finish line was just over a mile away—a white speck in the distance. Usually seeing the end of the race was enough for me to give it a final kick but fatigue had settled in. My arms hung limply at my sides and my shoulders felt tight. I wanted to glance behind me and see how close the second-place runner was but that went against all my training. I fought the temptation and focused on the finish.

A spectator stepped into the road and started running alongside me. I was so exhausted that it took me a moment to realize it was my dad.

"You're in first place!" he said, his voice filled with a combination of excitement and pride.

"How close is the next runner?" I said. It took all of my energy and concentration to force the words out of my mouth.

My dad glanced over his shoulder. "I don't see her," he said.

Was he serious? Did I really have a chance to win a marathon? A surge of excitement and energy surged through me.

"I can do this," I said to my dad. "I can win it."

"You sure?"

"See you at the end," I said.

My dad pulled off and I focused on the finish line. I gave the last mile everything I had. The race was no longer about qualifying for Boston or a three-hour finish. It was all was about winning. This was a once-in-a-lifetime opportunity, and nothing would stop me from coming in first. I focused on the finish line and ran faster. The temptation to look over my shoulder vanished.

Five minutes later I won the Ogden Marathon with a time of three hours, six minutes, and forty-eight seconds. I placed my hands on the back of my head and leaned over to catch my breath. Mentally, I was elated. Physically, I was drained. Those feelings merged into an exhausted euphoria that made me want to celebrate and collapse simultaneously.

"Julie, you did it! You won! You won!"

Across the barrier that separated the runners from the crowd, I saw my dad. Sweat beaded his brow but he had a huge smile on his face. I walked over and hugged him over the barrier. His strong arms nearly lifted me off the ground.

"What a finish!" he said. "That was amazing!"

If I was to give credit to anyone else for my victory, it would be my dad. Without his support on Saturday mornings, I never would have trained hard enough to win.

"Thanks for all your love and support," I said. "I couldn't have done it without your help."

Other familiar cheers and voices filled the air as my mom and three younger sisters came up to congratulate me. It made my victory much sweeter knowing my family was there. The only person missing was Brian. Last week he'd said the race was too early for him to be there in person, but he would meet me at his parents' home later in the day. After I had time to rest and recover, the plan was to spend the afternoon together. I agreed, but after winning, I wished he was there to celebrate. I didn't dwell on that thought long. Instead, I savored the moment and everything I had accomplished.

I grabbed a bottle of cold water, an orange, and a banana and made my way out of the runners' area to spend time with my family. I wanted to go home, shower, and rest, but there was an award ceremony, and as the winner, I needed to attend. While I cooled down, they posted official times. I finished my bottle of water and looked at the results. Though I hadn't hit my three-hour goal, I had qualified for the Boston Marathon. I also won the race by thirty seconds.

After the ceremony, I drove home with a winner's medal around my neck and white flecks of salt on my face and arms. I took a long, hot bath, changed into sweats, and laid on my bed. I tried reading the latest Michael Connelly novel, but I didn't finish the first page before falling asleep.

When I woke up two hours later, my body had stiffened—an early preview of tomorrow's aches and pains. However, the nap had given me enough strength to drive to Layton. I didn't know what Brian had planned, but I hoped it didn't involve movement. I curled my hair and put on some makeup before heading out the door.

Brian's parents lived in a comfortable middle-class home on the east side of the city near the mountains. His tan Honda Accord was in the driveway. Before I rang the doorbell, Brian opened the door and flashed a big smile.

"You won!" he said and gave me a hug, his strong arms nearly pushing the breath out of me.

How had he known about my victory? Had my dad called and told him?

As if reading the confusion on my face, Brian said, "They posted the results online."

I didn't know my time would be on the internet, but was glad Brian had looked it up. Talking up my accomplishments is hard because it feels like bragging. If he hadn't looked up the results, I would have told him I qualified for Boston and left it at that.

"Are you hungry?" Brian asked.

I hadn't eaten since finishing the race, and the mention of food made my stomach rumble.

"Starving," I said.

"Let's get some food, and you can tell me about your win."

We ate at a nearby Chinese restaurant. Over orange chicken and Mongolian beef, I recapped the run. Afterward, we returned to his parents' house, and Brian suggested we watch a movie. Normally I preferred to do anything besides sitting, but today doing nothing was exactly what I needed. We cuddled on a comfortable leather couch in the basement, and I sank into the soft cushions. The movie started and I rested my head on

Brian's shoulder. Soon I dozed off. When I woke up, my head still rested on Brian, and the credits rolled on the screen. I sat up, stretched my arms, and yawned.

"You were really tired," Brian said.

"I shouldn't be," I replied. "I napped before coming over here."

"Well, you ran twenty-six miles."

"Twenty-six point two," I said. "The extra two-tenths of a mile really does you in."

Brian laughed and said, "When are we going to see each other again?"

"Why don't you come to church with me tomorrow?" I suggested.

"I forgot to bring a shirt and tie with me," he said. "Why don't you drive to Provo and we can go together?"

If I hadn't run a marathon, I might have agreed, but knowing how sore my body would be tomorrow, sitting in the car was the last thing I wanted to do. I thought about asking Brian to make a quick trip to the mall together so we could pick something up or tell him to borrow some clothes from his family, but I was too tired to have that discussion again.

"My sore body won't make the drive to Provo," I said.

"Don't worry," he said. "We'll make it work another Sunday."

We switched topics. Before I left, we made plans to get together in Ogden the following Saturday. I was too exhausted to be disappointed that, once again, I'd be attending church alone.

CHAPTER TEN

Abel

When I woke up on Sunday, my first thoughts were of Julianna. The miracle of the ward boundary change was still at the front of my mind, and I hoped she would be at church so I could take advantage of this second chance.

I scrambled some eggs and retrieved the newspaper from the porch. I pulled out the sports section and nearly dropped it on my breakfast. A large color photo of someone who looked like Julianna graced the front page. My eyes had to be playing tricks on me because that had to be Julianna's twin or doppelgänger. I inspected the photo. The woman wore a white singlet and purple shorts. A sheen of sweat covered her skin, and her face was scrunched in a determined look. I read the photo's caption. It really was Julianna Taylor. The woman who had occupied my thoughts for the last month and a half had won the Ogden Marathon.

As I stared at the photo in disbelief, the powerful, electric sensation once again surged through my body. The marathon and her victory gave me the perfect excuse to talk with her. I ate my eggs and headed back to my room to get ready for church.

Entering my bedroom, my eyes drifted to the photo of Krista, and I realized this was the first morning since her death that she wasn't my first thought. Rarely an hour went by without a memory, question, or thoughts of Krista passing through my mind. Yet today, until this moment, every waking thought was on Julianna. What did that mean in relation to Krista? I wasn't sure and didn't want to dwell on it. Still, the thought had dampened my excitement and reminded me that if I fell in love again, there were still issues I needed to work through.

I left early for church in hopes that a quiet, more spiritual location would settle my nerves. There were a handful of cars in the parking lot, but the chapel was dark, quiet, and empty. I turned on the lights and debated whether to take my usual seat at the back or sit near Julianna's usual spot. Would she show up? I'd never run a marathon, but had heard from runner friends how sore their bodies were following the race. Would Julianna be too physically uncomfortable to attend? I hoped not.

I opted for the back pew. Closing my eyes, I prayed and meditated. By the time the organist arrived to practice hymns, I was ready to talk with Julianna.

She arrived five minutes before the services began. She wore a white blouse and a tight black skirt that revealed enough of her long, slender legs to drive me crazy. Was it possible for her not to look beautiful? Apparently not. I spent the entire service refining what I'd say to her.

On her way to Sunday School Julianna walked noticeably slower. I waited a minute and followed her to class. My plan was to congratulate her on her victory after class and see if she wanted to discuss her training schedule. Class dragged. When it finally ended, my stomach clenched, and I heard my heart beating in my ears. I spotted my mom at the front of the room talking to another woman, and I hoped she wouldn't turn around. I wiped my hands on my pants and tapped Julianna on the shoulder.

"Congratulations on winning the marathon," I said.

Julianna's cheeks flushed red. She looked away for a moment before making eye contact again.

"Thanks," she said.

Her soft voice had a slight lilt. It was music to my ears.

"That was a great photo of you in the paper," I said.

Julianna's cheeks burned crimson. She looked unsure how to respond.

"I wasn't expecting that," she said.

Sensing she didn't want to discuss the photo, I steered the conversation back to running. "I'm a runner and would like to know more about your training schedule."

"Do you run marathons?" she said.

"No, but maybe I would after knowing what it takes to train for one."

The Sunday School room was filling with people, and the next meeting would start any minute. I needed to be in another class for the third hour of church. We had little time to talk.

"There's a social after church," I said. "We could talk more about running then."

"I don't attend socials," Julianna said.

I wasn't sure if she was brushing me off or being sincere, but I had to talk with her.

"I'm not a fan either," I replied. "We could talk elsewhere if you want."

Julianna bit her lower lip and nodded. "I'll see you at the social."

"My name's Abel," I said, extending my hand.

"I'm Julianna," she said, taking mine and shaking it.

"I know," I said. "Your picture was in the paper."

Julianna's cheeks flushed red for the third time.

I walked out of the room with a skip in my step and a smile across my face. The conversation had gone better than I expected. In an hour, I'd have another chance to get to know Julianna better. If all went well, we'd be going out that weekend.

CHAPTER ELEVEN

Julianna

    I shifted uncomfortably on my padded chair through the last hour of church. Pushing my body to its limits created aches and pains in places I'd never felt before. I wanted to stand up, stretch the muscles in my arms and legs then take a walk, but that wasn't possible. Instead, I extended, straightened, and rubbed one arm and leg at a time while remaining in my seat. It was an imperfect solution, but would get me through the last twenty minutes of class.

    My discomfort wasn't only physical. My gut told me Abel would ask me out at the social, and I debated whether to accept his invitation. Brian and I had never discussed being exclusive, but as far as I knew, he wasn't dating anyone else. Still, I felt more like a companion than a girlfriend. It would be easier to tell Abel I had a boyfriend if Brian had been at the finish line yesterday, or came to church with me occasionally. Perhaps it wouldn't hurt to go out once with someone else as a gut check.

I went back and forth on what to say, and by the time class ended, I had resolved to let fate determine whether to accept Abel's invitation—assuming he extended one. If he wanted to do something on Friday, the night I had no plans, I would accept. If he asked me out on Saturday, I'd tell him I already had a date.

When I arrived at the social, Abel wasn't there. My anxiety spiked. I don't enjoy attending large gatherings where I don't know many people. I assumed Abel would arrive before me and I wouldn't have to concern myself with striking up a conversation with strangers. I scanned the table laden with cookies, brownies, and other delicious-looking baked goods, but I was more nervous than hungry. I filled a plastic cup with water and stood along the far wall so I could see when Abel arrived.

By the time I finished my water, there was still no sign of Abel. I shifted my weight uncomfortably from one leg to the other. Standing didn't feel good. I wanted to lie down. I looked at my watch and gave Abel three minutes to show up. I could always give him running tips next week.

Abel arrived as I was about to head for the exit. He scanned the room and smiled when our eyes met. I didn't get a good look at him earlier, so I checked him out as he made a beeline toward me. He stood well over six feet tall, rail thin, with a high forehead. He wore dark-rimmed glasses, a white shirt, and a dark-blue tie that matched his eyes. He looked to be in his mid-twenties—older than me, but not by much. He didn't wear a wedding band.

We exchanged pleasantries, then Abel said, "Tell me about winning the marathon."

I felt heat on my cheeks and did my best to hold eye contact.

"I ran faster than anyone else," I said, unsure exactly what to say.

Abel laughed. "I know how it ended. Tell me about the race."

I gave Abel an abbreviated version of my run. When I finished, Abel asked about my training schedule. I gave him an overview of the mileage and dedication required to prepare for a twenty-six-mile race. Abel asked more questions. He made eye contact and nodded his head as I talked. I enjoyed having an in-depth conversation about running. Outside of my dad, I couldn't think of the last time I'd had such a detailed conversation on the topic. Maybe Abel really did want to run a marathon, and I had misread his intentions. My mind flashed back to chemistry study groups where guys had asked for help. I had thought, even hoped, that some of them were using chemistry to get to know me better. However, all they ever wanted was assistance with their homework.

In the background, the crowd was thinning, and since Abel didn't seem interested in asking me out, I looked for an excuse to leave.

"We should go running together," Abel said.

My stomach tightened. Was this Abel's way of asking for a date?

"I run four or five miles most mornings. You know, to stay in shape," Abel continued, patting his flat stomach. "If you want, we could run Friday after work. There's a beautiful four-mile course near my place."

Heat rushed to my cheeks, and the knot in my stomach tightened. Friday. Abel had asked me to run on a Friday. Fate had spoken.

"That sounds good. What time?" The words tumbled out of my mouth before I could stop them.

Abel gave me his address, and we agreed on a time to meet.

On the drive home, I realized that our conversation had focused entirely on me. Aside from running, I knew nothing about Abel. What else would I learn about him on Friday? Getting to know him better gave me something to look forward to.

•••

I didn't give Abel much thought the rest of the week. I did, however, note where he lived as I passed his home on my daily five-minute commute. His house was a small, boxy looking home with white and brown siding and wooden shingles. The blinds were always closed and the lights off. I never saw a car in the driveway.

Friday morning, I went on my scheduled training run. I still planned on running with Abel that afternoon, but assumed his pace wouldn't be close to my training speed. I wanted to relax during our run and talk—not run him into the ground. Besides, any additional miles I ran with Abel were a bonus. On the drive home from work, I noted that Abel's house was still dark.

I changed into running clothes and ran the mile to Abel's house, timing my departure to arrive at exactly at six o'clock. A hundred yards from his home, I saw a dark blue Dodge Neon in the driveway and a light on in the front room. It was the first time I had seen signs of life there.

Abel smiled when he opened the door. He wore blue running shorts and a white T-shirt with a tech logo on the left breast. He looked over my shoulder. "Did you run here?" he asked.

"Yes."

"Why didn't you drive?"

"I love running."

Abel invited me inside while he put on his running shoes. I stood just inside the door and looked around, hoping to learn a little more about him. A kitchen that looked recently remodeled was off to the right. There was a small dining area with a table and four matching chairs. To the left was a living room with a couch against one wall, a coffee table, and a small TV in a corner. On the coffee table stood an inch-high stack of magazines and a four-by-six photo of a blonde woman. The walls were white and bare. It was a well-furnished home for a single person in his twenties—especially the matching kitchen table and chairs.

Abel tied his shoes, and we started our run. He guided me through unfamiliar streets and neighborhoods of tall, mature trees that shaded the road. Even though Abel's eight-minute-per-mile pace was slower than my training run, it gave me time to take in my surroundings and talk. Between breaths, I told him about my job working analyzing drugs in the state crime lab. Abel summed up his job working as a copywriter for a super-computing company. The conversation flowed and things were going well enough that I hoped Abel would want to spend more time together when we finished.

"Does running make you hungry?" Abel asked as we sat on his front porch catching our breath and drinking tall, cold glasses of water.

"Yes," I said.

"Would you like to get something to eat? After we clean up, of course."

"I'd like that," I said.

Abel stood and took the empty glass from my hand.

"Want a ride home?" Abel asked.

"That's okay. I'll run," I said.

"You sure?"

"I'm a runner."

Abel said he'd pick me up in an hour. I ran the mile back to my apartment, showered, and got ready as fast as I could. I was starving and looked forward to a good meal and more conversation.

Right at the scheduled time, Abel knocked on my door. Being prompt is important to me, and the fact that he showed up on time meant a lot. Abel wore jeans and a navy-blue T-shirt that clung to his thin frame.

"Ready to eat?" he asked.

My stomach grumbled loud enough that I was sure Abel heard it.

"Yes, I'm hungry," I said.

We walked to his car and I stood by the passenger door, expecting Abel to open it. Instead, he got in the driver's side. I paused, unsure what to do. My dad said a guy should open the car door on a date. Even after twenty-seven years of marriage, it was something he always did for my mom. Abel didn't seem to notice that I was standing outside the car door waiting. Maybe this was something he didn't do. I gave him a pass and opened the door, but if there was a second date, Abel would have to know my expectations.

"There's a good restaurant up in Logan called the Bluebird," Abel said. "Want to eat there?"

Logan was a college town forty-five minutes to the north. My stomach grumbled in protest but I agreed, figuring the drive gave us more time to get to know each other. Our conversation picked up where it had left off, and we talked about our families and different places we'd lived over the years. I learned Abel grew up near the home he currently lived in and was the oldest of six kids—three boys and three girls. I told him about growing up in Tacoma, Washington, moving to Utah, and stories about being the second oldest in a family of seven girls.

"Do any of your siblings have kids?" I asked as the city of Logan came into view.

"One sister had her first child a couple months ago," Abel said. "A girl."

"So, she's your parents' first grandchild," I said. "They must be excited."

Abel took a long moment before answering. "Yeah," he said. "They are."

He switched the conversation back to my job, and I told him stories about interesting objects the police had brought in for me to analyze.

"Do you only identify drugs?" Abel asked.

"That's my primary job. I'm also training in serology."

"Serology?"

"Body fluids like blood and semen. Once I certify, I can analyze blood spatter or process rape kits."

"The lab sounds like a fascinating place to work. Much more interesting than my job."

"There's always something to learn," I said. "We have a gun range and a co-worker who does ballistic tests. He's taught me a lot about guns. You'd be amazed what a bullet can do to a human brain."

Abel bit his lower lip and then asked, "When did you move to Ogden?"

"January."

From his furrowed brow, Abel appeared to be calculating something in his head. "When did you start attending the ward?" he asked.

"Right after I moved in," I said, puzzled at the questions.

Abel rubbed his chin and seemed lost in thought, far away from the narrow road and lush green corn and alfalfa fields that filled this end of Cache County. Did I say something wrong? I replayed our conversation in my mind, but couldn't pinpoint anything out of the ordinary. If I had said something that bothered or offended him, I hoped he'd speak up.

Even at the late hour, the Bluebird was busy, but the server found us a table for two in the middle of the restaurant. I ordered chicken parmesan and Abel ordered a Reuben sandwich with a side of fries. Our conversation continued.

"What's your favorite part of your job?" I asked.

"Writing website copy is fun." He said the words to his plate instead of to me. He picked up his fork, stabbed at his fries, and set it back down.

"Do you see yourself doing that for a living?"

Abel placed his napkin on the table. "I don't know. Maybe. I'm learning HTML so I can code websites."

He answered the question, but I sensed his mind was elsewhere. Again, I wondered if I had said or done something wrong. Family, jobs, and hobbies had been the bulk of our conversation. We hadn't discussed politics, social issues, or anything controversial.

I took a sip of my water to buy a moment to think.

Abel opened his mouth, but quickly shut it. He looked over my shoulder then back at his plate. I turned to see what had caught his attention. Behind me were tables full of families and couples eating dinner. Nothing out of the ordinary.

"Do you think you're going to make a career out of the crime lab?" Abel said.

He spoke to the table instead of me.

"I don't know. To be honest, I'm considering going to medical school."

"Medical school?"

"You know, to be a doctor."

Abel nodded, but said nothing. Had he even heard what I said?

I didn't know what was going on, but maybe a few minutes of silence would help reset the evening. Halfway through my meal, I noticed that Abel had stopped eating. He picked at his fries again, a flat expression on his face. Before I could ask if there was a problem, he looked me in the eye and said, "I'm a widower. I lost my wife five months ago."

The bite of chicken parmesan slid down my throat like a rock. I looked at his right hand and didn't see a pale line on his ring finger. I waited for him to say more, but his eyes focused on his half-eaten sandwich.

While I waited in silence, I tried to guess his age. I didn't see any gray hair, crow's feet, fine lines, or wrinkles that showed he was much older than me. Twenty-six? Twenty-seven? Twenty-eight? How could someone that young be a widower? How long ago did he say his wife had died? Did he say how she died? How long were they married? Did Abel have any children? Despite the slew of questions flying through my mind, I didn't feel comfortable asking them. Abel had brought up, or more accurately, dropped his marital status like a bomb from a plane. He might as well hit me with anything else related to the subject. But it had to be on his terms, so I waited for him to offer more information.

Awkward silence engulfed our table. I looked at my food, no longer hungry. Abel finally said something, but instead of talking about him, he asked another question about my job. I didn't want to talk about drugs or lab equipment. I wanted to know more about him.

The conversation never recovered, and the forty-five-minute drive back to Ogden felt like an eternity. When we arrived, I let out a silent sigh of relief. Abel parked near my apartment, and I waited for him to either say something about being a widower or at the very least open my car door and walk me to my door. Aside from putting the car in park, Abel made no sign he was going to do either of these. Finally, I wished him goodnight, opened my door, and hurried to my apartment, relieved that the date was over.

Ten minutes later, I packed an overnight bag and headed out the door. Even though the date with Abel was a disaster, I looked forward to telling my family about it. Their groans, laughs, and sympathy would help ease the discomfort I felt from the worst date of my life.

I found my dad in the front room, sitting in his favorite chair reading a novel. My mom sat on the couch, brushing one of my little sisters' hair.

"You're here!" my dad said, sliding a bookmark between the pages and setting the book to the side.

"We were thinking you decided to run in Ogden tomorrow," my mom said.

"I had a date," I said. "It went late."

My mom stopped in mid brush. "With Brian?"

"No," I said. I set my overnight bag on the floor then sat on the opposite end of the couch from my mom.

"With who?" my dad asked.

"Some guy from church."

"I didn't think there were any single men in your ward."

"I didn't either," I said, though I wondered if being widowed was the same as being single.

"So, how'd it go?" my mom asked.

"Awful," I said. I recapped the evening, expecting everyone to roll their eyes, laugh, and tell me I dodged a bullet. I got that reaction from my mom but my dad sat quietly and listened.

"Sounds like that date could have gone better," he said when I finished.

"I wish he'd mentioned the widower thing before we went out," I said.

"Would you have turned him down?"

I opened my mouth to say something, but took a moment to collect my thoughts. I'd never considered dating a widower before. Widowers had gray hair, wrinkles, and drove Cadillacs. They weren't in their twenties, working at tech companies.

"I don't know," I admitted.

"Maybe this was his first date since his wife died," my dad said.

My dad's words gave me pause. If it was Abel's first date as a widower, his actions were a little more understandable. However, that didn't mean there'd be a second date. I had no interest in dating someone who was previously married.

"Maybe he'll mention his marital status *before* asking his next date out," I said.

"You know, Julie," my dad said, "maybe you should give him a second chance."

"Steve!" my mom said, her voice full of astonishment.

My dad's words stunned me into silence. Was he serious? I waited for him to smile or say he was joking, but his face remained sober. Where had this idea come from? My dad always emphasized the high standards my sisters and I should expect from the men we dated. Abel didn't treat me poorly, but his lack of communication was awful. Besides, dating a widower brought up questions and issues I didn't want to think about. Was Abel sealed to his wife? If he married again, would he have two wives in the next life? Would he and his two wives share a heavenly mansion? A heavenly bed? I shook those thoughts from my mind. None of that mattered because I wasn't going out with him again.

I must have had a concerned look on my face because my dad said, "You can do what you want, Julie. I just thought a second date might go better."

It certainly couldn't be any worse, I thought.

"Are you going to go out with him again?" my mom asked.

"I don't know," I said shrugging my shoulders. I was too tired to think about it.

I excused myself and headed to bed, ready to put this day behind me. Pulling the covers around my neck, I realized Abel would probably be at church on Sunday. If I hadn't been in such a hurry to leave, I would have packed some Sunday clothes and gone to church with my family or Brian. I tossed and turned, debating whether to borrow some of my sisters' clothing or bite the bullet and go to church in Ogden. Finally, I decided I couldn't hide from Abel forever, so I might as well get it over with. The decision made, I drifted off into a fitful sleep.

CHAPTER TWELVE

Abel

After my date with Julianna, I drove home feeling like I'd been sucker-punched in the stomach. My world felt shaky and unstable, and I found it difficult to breathe. Julianna wasn't my first bad date since being widowed but I'd shrugged them off as learning experiences or even laughed about them after. I couldn't just brush my date with Julianna to the side. From the moment she showed up at my house, I felt a special connection. It was more than the proverbial sparks that some people described after meeting someone for the first time. With Julianna it started as a flame and by the end of the evening, it had turned into a raging bonfire. The intensity of these feelings made my mistakes and missteps extra agonizing. I had assumed she knew about my marital status, like everyone at church. When I realized she didn't know about Krista, I panicked and blurted it out during dinner.

In bed I stared at the ceiling and replayed the date in my mind, wishing I could get a do-over. Since my mind was buzzing with all the things that went wrong, I turned on the bedside lamp and picked up a novel, hoping to distract myself, but I couldn't concentrate. Finally, I gave up and returned to staring at the ceiling.

At some point my eyes wandered to the eight-by-twelve photo of Krista above my dresser. It was her college graduation picture taken six months after we tied the knot. As a first-generation college graduate, Krista wanted to commemorate her accomplishment with something visible. The photo sent me down a rabbit hole of college-related memories: late night study sessions in the library, working at the writing center, a school-sponsored trip to the University of Arizona, and upper division English classes—all things we did together. The memories triggered a sense of excitement and connection; feelings I experienced dating Krista, and later, as newlyweds.

Was it possible to have that connection again with someone else?

I didn't believe in soulmates. The notion that you could fall in love with only one person in this lifetime didn't resonate with me. Instead, I believe each of us have several people we feel drawn to in a soulful way; people with whom we can live a long, happy life together. The challenge was to find one of them. Krista was one. When we first started spending time together in the college library, I connected with her on a level I didn't know was possible. She was my ideal complement. Within a month of dating, I knew I could happily be with her for the rest of this life and all of eternity. As our relationship matured, these feelings only grew stronger.

After a year of dating, I had a decision to make: ask Krista to marry me or serve a two-year mission for the Church of Jesus Christ of Latter-day Saints. If I chose the latter there was no guarantee Krista would wait. When we started going out, she had been writing a missionary who she had seriously dated before he left for his mission to Mexico. After we became exclusive, she had penned a breakup letter. Her beauty and personality attracted men like bees to nectar and I knew they'd line up to ask her out once I left. I also had several friends who'd left waiting girlfriends behind only to receive "Dear John" letters within a year. Despite expressing and showing her love for me, twenty-four months was a long time and I knew the odds of Krista waiting were slim.

I loved Krista. I wanted to marry her. So, deciding whether or not to leave on a mission was challenging. I spent a lot of time on my knees praying, reading scriptures, and considering my options. Ultimately, I knew I needed to serve a mission. Part of what helped me reach that decision was my belief that if Krista didn't wait, I would meet another "right fit." Or so I hoped. Leaving on a mission was an act of faith. I returned home elated and relieved that Krista had waited. Our relationship picked up where it left off and a year after my return, we married in the Logan Temple.

Could I rekindle that same love and devotion with someone else? I didn't want to spend the rest of my life alone, but I wasn't sure I'd find someone who made me feel at home with myself. Using Julianna or any other woman as a placeholder was unfair to both of us. Waking up next to someone I didn't love was worse than spending the rest of my life widowed. If I married again, I wanted it to be for the right reasons and not to fill the gaping hole in my heart.

I thought about love, connection, marriage, and eternal relationships until my eyes grew heavy. When I finally drifted off to sleep, I didn't know if I'd ever be able to love someone as much as I loved Krista.

•••

The next morning, I went for a run, hoping that exercise would clear my head and help me figure out how to make things right with Julianna. While retracing the four-mile route we had run the day before, I crafted an apology. I arrived home hot and sweaty, drank a glass of cold water, and jotted down what I'd say to her at church tomorrow.

I took my time showering. I let the hot water wash away the sweat, grime, and emotional weight from the previous evening. I stayed in the shower until the water turned lukewarm.

Back in my bedroom, as I toweled my hair dry, a Krista-related memory infiltrated my mind. Since her death, unsolicited memories happened on a daily basis. A trip to the grocery store might trigger scenes from our budget-constrained shopping trips, while driving past a restaurant could bring back recollections of a fun night on the town. Seeing the well-worn spine of a book could spark thoughts of late-night study sessions or browsing a bookstore. A whiff of Krista's perfume instantly transported me to intimate moments we shared.

There was no way to predict when a memory might occur or what emotion it would invoke. I don't know what triggered this memory. Maybe it had something to do with coming out of the shower, seeing the unmade bed and wishing Krista was in it. Whatever the reason, a forgotten memory forced its way to the forefront of my mind.

It was a hot summer morning, and I had just gotten out of the shower. The air conditioning had never worked well in our apartment and I walked into our bedroom naked, enjoying the cool sensation.

Krista stirred as I dressed. She sat up and rubbed the sleep from her eyes.

"I had the strangest dream," she said.

"Yeah?" I said as I slid on my jeans. I was only halfway listening. I had to leave for work in ten minutes and my thoughts were on getting dressed and grabbing a quick bite before heading out the door.

"I dreamed I met your future wife," Krista said.

"Future wife?" I said, not sure if I heard her right.

"Yes, your future wife."

I grabbed a T-shirt from a drawer, pulled it over my head and said, "Last I checked, we're married. You're my wife. There is no future wife."

Krista shook her head. "No, this was different. In the future I think you're going to marry someone else."

I gave Krista a why-are-you-telling-me-this look. Did she want reassurance that I loved her? I grabbed a pair of socks and sat next to her on the bed as I pulled them on.

"It was only a dream," I said.

I expected Krista to lean her head on my shoulder while I told her she was the love of my life. Instead, she brushed the hair out of her eyes and leaned forward.

"This was more than a dream," she said. "It was different . . . more powerful. I—I don't know how to describe it. I've never experienced anything like this. It was so . . . real."

I didn't know what to say. Krista and I had been married for six months. We were still in the honeymoon stage of our marriage, learning the ins and outs that came with living together. Did all women have dreams like this? Was this one of those husband things you had to figure out? Was it related to concerns some Latter-day Saint women had about eternal polygamy? Finally, I sputtered, "Do you know her? What did she look like?"

Krista shrugged. "I didn't see her face. She was looking away from me. She wore a gorgeous white dress and had curly, light-colored hair that went halfway down her back. It was only the two of us in this beautiful, white room with high ceilings. I wanted to say something to her but I couldn't open my mouth. While I looked at her, I had this strong impression that at some point you were going to marry this woman and that I was okay with it."

I glanced at the clock on the nightstand next to the bed. I needed to be out the door in five minutes and hadn't eaten yet. "I'm not planning on marrying this mystery woman or anyone else," I said. "It won't happen even if the church brings back polygamy."

Krista opened her mouth to say something but shut it. Her shoulders slumped and she looked down at the covers. Whatever I should have said, that wasn't it.

"I've never had a dream this intense before," she said quietly.

"And you probably won't have another one," I said. I took her hands and kissed the top of her head. "You're the perfect woman for me. I don't want or need anyone else."

Krista gave me a half smile—her way of telling me there was no point continuing the conversation if I wouldn't take it seriously.

"I love you," I said.

"I love you, too," she replied.

I gave her another kiss, this one on the lips, and hurried to the kitchen to get something to eat.

We never spoke about her dream again.

Years later, I searched through old journals, unsure if my memory about her dream or being so dismissive was right. I found the day, though most of what I wrote about had to do with frustration about my job and Krista's parents. I only wrote three lines about her dream and described it as "crazy" though I wondered if I had said or done something that triggered her insecurities.

Back in my room, I sat on my bed as the memory replayed on a loop in my mind.

"I wish I could talk with you," I said, looking at Krista's photo on the wall. "I wish you were here to explain that dream and a bunch of other things to me."

Krista smiled back at me from her photograph.

She said nothing.

CHAPTER THIRTEEN

Julianna

To minimize any chance of talking to Abel, I purposely timed my arrival at church minutes before the service began. My normal pew was empty. I took my seat and resisted the urge to see if Abel was in attendance. I didn't want to make eye contact. Still, I needed to know where he was. During a prayer, I opened my eyes and quickly scanned the congregation, spotting him on the back row of the chapel. My stomach clenched. I considered making a beeline for my car as soon as sacrament meeting ended and missing the rest of church, but decided that running away from Abel would only delay the inevitable. If we needed to talk, I might as well get it over with.

The service ended, and I headed straight to Sunday School. I didn't see Abel. Class started and there was no sign of him. Maybe Abel felt as awkward as I did about the date and skipped class or went home early like I'd planned to. The tension in my gut lessened as the prospects of running into him diminished.

After church, I weaved through the packed hallways toward the exit. I looked for his tall, lanky frame, but there was no sign of him. By the time I reached the parking lot, I thought I had avoided him. Halfway to my car, however, I heard one of the side doors of the church open, followed by hurried footsteps. Before I could turn around, I heard Abel's voice.

"Julianna, wait!"

I glanced over my shoulder. Abel hurried after me, his tie flopping from side to side like a dying fish. It felt like I had swallowed a twenty-pound weight. I didn't want to talk to Abel, but told myself that this conversation needed to happen. I kept walking to my car to minimize the time we had to talk. In a moment, Abel walked beside me, matching me step for step.

"Do you want to go out again this weekend?" he said, his words coming out in a rushing gasp.

His boldness caught me off guard. I expected an apology or explanation, not an invitation. Confused, it took me a moment to gather my thoughts. For some unknown reason, my dad's suggestion about giving Abel a second chance popped into my mind.

"Sure," I said. The word spilled out of my mouth before I could stop it.

Abel lost a pace in his step, as if my answer surprised him. Almost to my vehicle, I pressed the key fob, and with a chirp, the driver's side door unlocked. By then Abel had recovered and was next to me.

"How about a baseball game on Friday? I'll pick you up at six."

"Perfect," I said. "See you then."

I got in my car, stunned at my own words. Driving away, I glanced in the rearview mirror long enough to see Abel standing in the middle of the parking lot, his mouth agape.

What on earth had I agreed to?

•••

For the rest of the week, I questioned my decision. I didn't oppose giving Abel, or anyone else, a second chance. Far from it. If I'd had a bad date, I would appreciate a shot at redemption. However, Abel was a widower, and that problem couldn't be solved by a fun night out. I didn't want to be a second wife in this life or the next. While I relished the idea of spending eternity with the man I loved, I wanted my future husband's entire heart. The possibility of sharing anyone with another woman, alive or dead, turned my stomach.

Polygamy—or plural marriages, as the Church refers to them—are a well-known part of the Latter-day Saint faith and history. The Church banned earthly polygamy over a hundred years ago and any who practiced it after that point were excommunicated. But I also understood that widowers could be sealed to another woman, a heavenly form of polygamy. I have always been grateful that polygamy is no longer performed here on earth and hadn't given it much more thought until my date with Abel. If we got married, what would that mean for me in this life or the next one? That question swirled around my mind, but instead of dwelling on it, I dismissed it. This second date with Abel was a courtesy, a chance to learn about his wife and their marriage, and cement the fact that dating a widower wasn't for me. No matter how it turned out, there would not be a third one.

While combing my hair and putting on makeup Friday evening, I came up with a list of questions to ask Abel. How long was he married? How did his wife die? What were her likes and interests? Did I look anything like her? What temple were they sealed in? As I pulled my ponytail through the back of a baseball cap, I pictured Abel breaking down in the middle of the date as he answered my questions. At that moment, I realized it was possible that our second date could turn out worse than the first.

Abel arrived right at six. He wore knee-length jean shorts, a T-shirt, and a navy-blue baseball hat embroidered with a white English D. He smiled and said, "You look nice. Ready for some baseball?"

I blushed at his compliment.

"I'm ready," I said.

I cared little for baseball. Though I understood the skill involved, it never seemed like a real sport to me because the players spent most of their time standing around doing nothing. But since there wouldn't be much action on the field, that meant Abel and I would have plenty of time to talk—hopefully without tears.

The baseball stadium, located in the heart of Ogden, provided a beautiful view of downtown and the mountains. The ballpark was half full, and there were empty seats on either side of us. I hoped this would make it easier for the two of us to talk since there was little chance that strangers would listen in. Unfortunately, our conversation was as slow as the game. Mostly we sat in silence, exchanging words as often as the action on the field. When we talked, it was more about our jobs, what we studied in school, and our families. Occasionally Abel mentioned something he found interesting about the game. Though I learned a few new tidbits about Abel, he shared nothing about his wife or marriage.

What was your wife's name? Why are you dating so soon after her death? Were you sealed in the temple? Do you still love her? Am I anything like her? Even without my shyness, they were hard questions to ask, but I still thought Abel should address them. After all, he had asked me out.

Several times, I considered jump-starting a conversation by saying something like "So, tell me about your wife," but I pulled back at the last minute, worried that the question might prompt a tearful reaction. After our first date, I couldn't think of a more awkward moment than dropping the widower bomb in the middle of dinner, but having a man crying about his dead wife at a baseball game would have been worse. A lot worse. Besides, using the phrase "your wife" sounded odd. It felt like something a mistress would ask her lover.

When the game mercifully ended two and a half hours later, I'd learned nothing about Abel's deceased wife or marriage. I was frustrated at him for not saying anything and mad at myself for not speaking up. The only upside of our time together was that Abel opened my car door and walked me to my apartment. That was progress. There was no mention of a third date.

That night, I said a silent prayer of gratitude that even though my questions went unanswered, Abel hadn't broken down in tears while we were together. That, in my mind, was a win.

CHAPTER FOURTEEN

Abel

The morning after the baseball game, I woke up angry at Krista. Being furious at her was a daily occurrence. However, it was unusual for me to have these feelings first thing in the morning. Normally my anger manifested itself as the day unfolded, when something frustrating happened like a traffic jam on the commute to work or another hospital bill arriving in the mail. It would take years to realize that anger was my way of grieving. Instead of tears, I expressed my sorrow through channeled fury.

This morning, the source of my rage was my date with Julianna. Though not as bad as our first one, it was still awful. There were long pauses in our conversation, and when we spoke, there was a cardboard-like stiffness to our words. I blamed it on Krista. She had been an invisible third wheel the entire evening, a ghostly presence that neither of us acknowledged. Several times, I considered saying something to Julianna about Krista but had stopped myself, unsure exactly what to say or how to broach the subject. The other women I dated had eventually asked about Krista or our marriage, and I thought Julianna would say something that would give me an opening. But that didn't happen. Instead, she kept her attention focused on the field, talking occasionally, and looking uncomfortable. Maybe she didn't want to discuss my past or was unsure what to say. Ultimately, the reason didn't matter. I blew my second chance with her, and I doubted there would be a third.

If you hadn't killed yourself, I wouldn't be in this situation, I thought, clenching my fists and grinding my teeth. I thought a few more choice words before my rage reached its crescendo.

I hate you! I hate you! I hate you! I thought those words repeatedly until I was too tired to continue.

Usually, these feelings faded away once the source of my frustration disappeared, but this morning my anger continued to smolder. Apparently getting over a bad date with Julianna wasn't as easy as waiting for a traffic jam to clear.

I decided the best way to reset my feelings was exercise. I changed into running clothes and went for a six-mile run around the perimeter of the business depot near my home. It was Saturday, and the roads were quiet. Because the streets were empty and I didn't have to dodge cars, I pushed myself to complete the course in record time. I arrived home an hour later physically exhausted and too tired to be mad at Krista or upset at the blown date with Julianna. Mission accomplished.

I drank a glass of cold water and planned out the rest of my day. Aside from some grocery shopping, I had little to do. There were no dates, no planned activities with friends or family, or anything else to occupy my time. While I didn't mind some downtime, I did better when I kept busy. Having nothing to do was a recipe for dwelling on the bad date with Julianna and getting angry at Krista all over again.

I checked LDSsingles for new matches. Maybe there was someone I could connect with for a last-minute date. It had been nearly a week since I last logged in. I hoped there would be one or two new matches to explore, but it only showed the same faces I had seen a week ago. I had already messaged or gone out with all of them.

I was about to power down the computer when I wondered if Julianna had an online profile. She seemed too confident to resort to online dating, but I really didn't know that much about her. I updated my search filters, something I had only tweaked since first setting up my account, to find women who were logical, athletic, and liked to read. I clicked search and ten new faces appeared on the screen. Julianna wasn't one of them. I read through the profiles of the most attractive matches and wondered what it would be like to spend my life with a woman whose personality and interests were so different from Krista's.

Different from Krista. The words thundered through my head. *Different from Krista. Different from Krista. Different from Krista.*

It occurred to me that I had set my search filters to find women who were more or less like Krista—outgoing, vivacious, creative, tall, and blonde. Maybe there was no spark with the women I met through this site because I was subconsciously trying to find another Krista.

But there was only one Krista. If I wasn't expecting someone to have Krista-like qualities, would it be easier to feel a connection? Whoever I dated, I had to accept her for who she was—not who I wanted or wished her to be. My thoughts returned to Krista. I felt regret and remorse for the anger and words I'd expressed earlier and decided a trip to the cemetery would be a good way to make amends and think.

Krista's resting place was Evergreen Memorial Park—a new cemetery in the northeast corner of Ogden. It was a five-minute drive from my home and provided sweeping views of northern Weber County and on a clear day, the Great Salt Lake. As my tires crunched on the gravel drive, I noted I had the entire place to myself.

Next to Krista and Hope's headstone was a Mason jar filled with wilted daylilies. About every other visit, I found flowers or other tokens left by previous visitors, a reminder that others still grieved her loss. A jar of flowers was something my mom usually left. I moved the jar to the side, sat next to the headstone, and looked over the valley. At first, I enjoyed the sun's warmth and took in the view. The air was clear enough that I could spot the brown hump of Fremont Island amid the salty waters of the Great Salt Lake. Because the cemetery had no above-ground headstones, I would sometimes forget that there were dead people buried nearby. Today, it felt like I was sitting on a grassy hill.

At some point, my thoughts drifted to Krista. I remembered our first kiss, our wedding day, and the evening she told me she was pregnant. I calculated that Hope would be seven months old if she had lived, and imagined how the three of us would spend a warm summer Saturday together. My smile faltered, and I wiped a tear with the back of my hand. I snapped myself back to the present. This morning had already been a roller coaster of emotions, and I didn't want to revisit that path.

On the road below, a Saturn sedan—the same make and model as Julianna's—sped past the cemetery. Seeing the car changed the focus of my thoughts from what might have been to the future and whether I'd get another chance with Julianna.

For the next few minutes, my thoughts pinged back and forth like a metronome between the past and the present, between Krista and Julianna. Amid these thoughts, I realized my feelings had evolved beyond dating and longing for companionship. I wanted to get married again and start a family again with someone. And though I couldn't explain why, I hoped that person would be Julianna.

I placed a hand on Krista's headstone, hoping for some kind of reassurance or sign that Krista was okay with me opening my heart to someone else.

I felt nothing.

CHAPTER FIFTEEN

Julianna

    A week after our second date, Abel asked me out. Once again, I let fate decide if it would happen. Brian and I had plans for Saturday night, leaving Friday open again. Just like the first time, Abel asked if I wanted to have dinner with him Friday evening. I agreed because I felt bad for Abel and didn't want to hurt his feelings. Besides, maybe I'd learn more about Abel's wife and marriage. Though I didn't see a future together, my scientific mind was curious why Abel was dating so soon after her death.

    My first real insight to his past life finally came after dinner. After eating at a local pizzeria, Abel invited me back to his place for a movie. The conversation at the restaurant had been just as stiff and uncomfortable as our first two dates, but I agreed to the movie out of pure curiosity about what clues the house might hold. I had glimpsed the living room and kitchen area on our first date, but hadn't paid attention to the details. This was my opportunity to learn more.

I followed Abel inside. The kitchen and living room looked the same as the first time I saw them—clean and spartan.

"Would you like to see the rest of the house?" Abel asked.

"Of course," I said, hoping he would finally open up.

Abel had repurposed the first bedroom into a workout/laundry room. A washer and dryer took up most of the closet, and a weight bench filled in the middle of the room. Stacked along the far wall were Olympic-sized weights. What caught my attention was a framed photo of Abel and a woman. The woman, who looked to be in her early twenties, had a narrow face, high cheekbones, light blue eyes, and shoulder-length hair the color of the sun. She had a wide smile, and her happiness practically radiated off the picture. This had to be Abel's deceased wife. Abel also had a big smile, and looked a few years younger.

I hoped Abel would notice my interest in the photograph, but he continued down the hall, seemingly unaware that I had stopped. Seeing the woman I thought to be Abel's deceased wife piqued my curiosity. What was she like? Was her personality as radiant and bubbly as she seemed in the photograph? What had initially attracted Abel to her? Would I get along with her in heaven? The last question stopped me cold. Why was I thinking that? I wasn't sharing my future husband with any other woman—living or dead.

I caught up with Abel at the end of the hall. He showed me his office, which contained a computer, a desk, bookshelves, and a pile of packing boxes that was stacked neatly in one corner. The walls were white and bare. His bedroom was directly across the hall and contained a full-sized bed and a chest of drawers.

My attention snagged on a second photograph of Abel and the blonde woman. In this photo, they sat next to each other on white plastic lawn chairs. Her face was mostly buried in Abel's arm and chest, but based on what I could see—her jawline, high cheekbones, and yellow hair—she was the woman from the first photo. Abel wore a white shirt, tie, and slacks and leaned his head against hers.

The tour concluded but Abel said nothing about the photos or the woman. Abel had to be aware that I'd seen them. Shouldn't he say something? After all, he had invited me back to his place and offered the tour. But Abel only asked if I'd seen the movie he'd rented.

Frustrated, I sat on the far end of the couch and crossed my arms, hoping Abel would read my body language and stay as far away from me as possible. As Abel fiddled with the VCR, I noticed a four-by-six framed photograph on the coffee table of the same blonde woman. This one was more casual. She wore jeans and a T-shirt, and her hair was in a ponytail.

Instead of watching the movie, I spent the next ninety minutes sitting in uncomfortable silence. It was a surreal experience to be on a date with someone and having a photo of the person's wife staring back. From time to time, I glanced at the photo, searching for physical similarities between the two of us. Relieved there weren't any obvious ones, I wondered which of my physical characteristics Abel found attractive. Perhaps he was lonely and looking for companionship and had only asked me out because we attended the same church. I hoped this wasn't the case.

After the movie ended, Abel drove me home. It was a relief to be away from the photos and unanswered questions. As I packed an overnight bag, my frustration boiled over. The date had ended with even more questions about Abel's marriage, wife, and past life, and he still seemed unwilling to broach the topic. I didn't know if Abel would ask me out again, but if he did, I would tell him we couldn't see each other anymore. I couldn't date or have a relationship with someone who was unable to communicate.

•••

The next morning, I ran thirteen miles. Afterward, I took my usual spot on the trampoline with a paperback and chocolate milk. I finished my drink and lay on my back and called Brian. The plan was for him to drive to my parents' house, where we'd spend the rest of the day together.

Brian answered on the third ring. His voice sounded tired, like he had just woken up. After exchanging pleasantries and talking about my run, I asked him when he was driving down.

"I'm exhausted," he said. "I was up till two to make a work deadline."

I glanced at my watch. It was ten a.m.

"What if we meet at the south end of the valley for lunch?" This would cut his drive by twenty minutes and still give us plenty of time to spend together.

Brian let out a long breath. "I don't know," he said. "Maybe you could drive down here after you've cleaned up. I should be up and going by then."

For the next five minutes, we went back and forth as we tried to work out where and when to meet. In the end, we agreed that this weekend wasn't going to work out and we'd make plans to see each other next week.

After the call, I stared at the spotless blue sky. My stomach felt tight, and I needed a few minutes to unwind. While I waited for my body to relax, my mind whirled. *It shouldn't be a struggle to spend the afternoon together,* I thought. *If neither of us is willing to put in the effort to see each other, why are we dating?*

For the first time, I seriously considered ending things with Brian. I believe when you love someone, you should want to spend time with that person and be willing to make sacrifices for it to happen. If getting out of bed was too difficult for him and the drive to Provo was too much for me, what else would we find too hard or demanding as we continued dating? It didn't seem like we were setting ourselves up for long-term success.

Finally, I tucked my novel under my arm and headed inside to shower. In the kitchen, my dad was scrambling eggs for a breakfast sandwich. The air smelled like bacon and toast.

"Everything okay?" he asked.

No, everything was not okay, but I didn't want to get into it at the moment.

"I'm fine."

"When's Brian coming over?"

"He's not."

There must have been an edge to my words because my dad raised his eyebrows. I was too physically and emotionally drained to discuss it. I needed a long shower and some time to think.

"I'll fill you in later," I said.

"You headed back to Ogden?"

"Yes, after I clean up."

"Why don't you spend the night? Lexie's birthday is tomorrow. It will save you a trip."

Lexie was one of my younger sisters. As much as I enjoyed spending time with my family, I needed some time alone, and the best place for that was my apartment.

"Thanks, but I need to head back. I'll drive down after church tomorrow," I said.

"You sure?"

"Yes, I'm sure."

I sensed that my dad wanted to probe further, but he just nodded and returned to making breakfast.

On the drive home, I felt that ending things with Brian was the best thing to do, then spent the rest of the day figuring out the kindest way to tell him it was over. In bed that night, still unsure what to say, I tossed and turned. I wanted the whole thing to be over. Finally, I fell asleep. The next morning, I was tired, but felt good about my decision to break up with him and decided to call him after my sister's birthday party.

Thoughts about the inevitable breakup had consumed so much of my thoughts that I didn't even think about Abel until I was on my way to church. I was glad I was heading to my parents' home right after the first hour because it would lessen the chance that we would run into each other. Maybe I could get away with one breakup conversation today instead of two. But that didn't happen. Abel caught up with me in the hallway right after the services ended.

"We need to talk," he said.

No kidding, I thought, then said to Abel, "I'm on my way to my sister's birthday. Can't do it right now."

"What about later today?"

"I'll call when I get back," I said, making a beeline for the door. My anxiety spiked. This day couldn't end soon enough.

•••

I considered calling Brian on the drive back to Ogden, but ultimately decided it would be better to do it at my apartment. Having an emotional conversation while driving wasn't the best idea. Instead, I planned out exactly what to say and how to say it.

At my apartment, I changed into jeans and a T-shirt and dialed Brian's number. Cell phone reception could sometimes be spotty in my apartment, so I sat on the stairs outside and hoped no one in the nearby apartments would overhear the conversation.

"Hey, babe," Brian said. "You usually call before church. How are you doing?"

"We need to have a talk," I said.

Tears streaked my cheeks when I ended the call ten minutes later. They were tears of heartbreak, relief, and a thousand other emotions. The relationship with Brian was over. He had taken the news better than I expected. He asked some questions, but didn't put up much resistance or try to win me back. I took this as a sign that the relationship wasn't as strong as either of us thought. I dabbed my eyes with a tissue and went inside to clean up. In the bathroom, I washed away my tears, the smeared mascara, and my built-up anxiety. But my stomach still churned. I needed to make one more phone call.

I considered ending things with Abel over the phone, but thought this conversation was better done in person. If we would be seeing each other every Sunday, I needed to make it clear where things stood. An in-person conversation would help ensure there were no misunderstandings or ambiguity. I called Abel and let him know I was home. He said he'd be right over.

While waiting, I checked myself in the mirror. Red, puffy eyes looked back at me. I put on a seldom-used pair of glasses to help hide the fact I'd been crying. I didn't want Abel thinking my tears had anything to do with him.

A few minutes later Abel knocked on my door.

You can do this, Julie, I told myself. *It will all be over soon.*

Abel wore jeans and a dark blue T-shirt that popped against his sun-kissed face. I invited him inside, and he took a seat on the edge of the couch. I sat in a chair across from him. Before I could say anything, Abel spoke.

"Why do you keep going out with me?" he said.

The question came as a surprise. While I thought about what to say, Abel continued, "Our dates have been . . . awful."

Though it felt good to have Abel confirm my feelings, it startled me to hear him acknowledge it.

"If they're not that good, why do you keep asking me out?" I replied.

Abel swallowed and looked me right in the eye. "Because there's something special about you."

My face flushed from the compliment. What did he find so special? Did I remind him of his dead wife? I hoped it was something else.

"What's special about me?"

"So far . . . everything."

The room felt like a furnace, and I didn't know how to respond. I broke eye contact. Special or not, there were no more dates in our future

"I can't date someone who can't communicate," I said after regaining my thoughts.

"What do you mean?"

What did I mean? Was he serious? "You dropped the widower bomb on me in the middle of dinner, since then you've said nothing about your wife or marriage."

Abel stroked his chin. "Fair enough," he said.

"How come you've never brought her up?" I pressed. "You've had plenty of opportunities."

"I wasn't sure what to say," Abel said. "Usually, my dates ask questions about my past and I answer them."

"I can't date someone who shies away from talking about hard things."

Abel bit his lower lip then said, "I don't know how to talk about any of this. I've never been a widower before."

I decided to throw him a lifeline. "Fine," I said. "Tell me about your wife."

Abel raised his eyebrows. "What do you want to know?"

What did I want to know? Was he serious? I wanted to know everything and nothing about her, but decided to start with the basics.

I said, "Why don't we start with her name? I don't even know that."

"Krista. Her name was Krista."

Krista. I put the name with the photos of the smiling blonde woman in Abel's home.

"When did she die?"

"November."

Seven months. That seemed like a fast turnaround for someone to date again. I wanted to ask Abel why he was dating so soon, but since we weren't going out anymore, I focused on other questions.

"How long were you married?"

"She died a month shy of our third anniversary."

"How did she die?"

"Suicide," Abel said quietly. "She killed herself."

My breath rushed out of my lungs, and I grappled for something to say. I'd assumed she died from an accident or illness. Suicide had never crossed my mind.

"I—I'm sorry," I sputtered. It felt like I had swallowed glue and the words came out slowly, one syllable at a time. I didn't know what else to say. I studied Abel's face. His eyes darted back and forth between me and the floor, and I wondered if he was struggling to keep his emotions in check. Should I keep asking him questions?

"Krista was seven months pregnant when she died." Abel said.

I was too stunned to speak. I had never heard of a pregnant woman killing herself. What words of comfort could you say to someone who lost both a wife and a child? It wasn't one loss Abel was grieving, but two. This made his situation more heartbreaking, and "I'm sorry" didn't cut it.

"My daughter's name was Hope," Abel continued. "She was born soon after her mother died. When it was obvious she would not live on her own, I took her off life support nine days after her birth."

Abel's words tumbled out of his mouth as if he wanted to spit them out before choking on them. Perhaps he was reluctant to talk about Krista because it was emotionally taxing. While that was understandable, how could I have a relationship with someone who couldn't discuss difficult things? I needed someone who felt comfortable talking with me about anything. In a moment of self-reflection, I realized the advice applied to me too. I'd had many opportunities on our three dates to ask Abel questions, and yet hadn't done so. How could I expect Abel to talk about his wife if I couldn't?

Abel locked eyes with me, as if waiting for the next question. Whatever feelings had kicked themselves to the surface, he had pushed them back down.

There was one last question I wanted to ask. It was an odd one to ask after learning about his deceased daughter, but it was something I needed to know.

"Were you and Krista sealed in the temple?"

Abel nodded. "Yes. We were married in the Logan Temple."

Slowly, I exhaled. Abel's answer came as a relief. While I could see myself possibly marrying a divorced man, I couldn't marry someone who was eternally sealed to another woman. I couldn't and wouldn't share my future husband—whomever he might be—with anyone else. There was no point in asking further questions. I had all the information I needed. It was time to let him know I couldn't go out with him again.

I tried to look Abel in the eye as I spoke, but I couldn't hold his gaze. Instead, I focused on his chest. "I can't do this," I said.

"Do what?"

"Date a widower. There are too many issues and unanswered questions."

"Like what?"

I wanted to tell Abel I wasn't into threesomes, that I wanted my future husband's whole heart, I couldn't compete with a ghost, and I didn't want to share him with another woman in this life or the next. Instead, I asked, "Do you still love Krista?"

Abel paused before saying, "Yes."

"I can't date a man who loves another woman," I said.

I made eye contact, trying to gauge his reaction to my words. He ran his hand through his hair and nodded. "Okay, I understand."

It felt like someone had opened a safety valve somewhere in my body, expelling all the built-up tension and anxiety. Abel understood. That meant there would be no more dates. It was finally over. I'd never have to worry Abel about these widower-related issues again.

"What if we were friends?" Abel asked.

Friends? What did that mean? Saying "Hi" to each other on Sunday? Sitting by me during Sunday School? If that was what he meant, I could live with it. Besides, that was a good way to let him down gently.

"Sure," I said. "We can be friends."

"Okay, friends," Abel said.

After a beat, he stood, and I walked him to the door. The conversation had gone better than expected. I felt emotionally exhausted and couldn't wait for Abel to leave so I could lie down and rest.

Sunlight and fresh air flooded the apartment as Abel opened the door. He hesitated and said, "Do you want to do something on Saturday as friends?"

I didn't see a problem since we were just going to be friends.

"Sure," I said.

Abel said he'd pick me up at five and left.

For a moment, I stood in stunned silence, trying to figure out what I had agreed to.

A date? No, we had agreed to be friends, and friends didn't date each other. Maybe Abel was lonely and needed someone to hang out with occasionally. Why had I accepted his offer? My mind had said "no," but my mouth had said the opposite. The words had practically tumbled out. Perhaps things would be different without the pressure and expectations that came with dating. Maybe we could have fun as friends.

CHAPTER SIXTEEN

Abel

I drove home stunned that Julianna had agreed to go out mere moments after the friend talk. Asking her to be friends was intentional. As she had expressed her concerns about dating a widower, I didn't know what to say. I thought agreeing to be "friends" would buy me some time to address her concerns. Her body language—arms folded and sitting on the opposite end of the couch—indicated she didn't want anything to do with me.

Asking her out was something I'd felt prompted to do right before walking out the door. I didn't know why she'd agreed, but my gut told me our upcoming date, if you could call it that, was my last chance to make things work. But how could I overcome her worries about my love for Krista? Julianna's words weighed heavily on my mind. Logically, I understood her feelings. I couldn't marry a woman who still loved another man. Why should I expect her to feel different?

Back at home, I glimpsed the framed photograph of Krista on the coffee table. I loved the impromptu nature of the photo and how it captured Krista's cheerful personality. I smiled every time I looked it. I took two steps toward my bedroom and stopped, recalling how Julianna had leaned against the far end of the couch on our last date. At the time, I thought she was putting as much space as possible between the two of us, but now I wondered if Krista's photograph had something to do with it too. I picked up the photo. The cheap plastic frame felt heavy in my hand. If things moved forward with Julianna, I needed to make room in my heart for her. Though I didn't know how to go about that, at the very least I could make my living room a place where she felt comfortable.

I tapped the frame against my palm and walked through the house, looking for a more suitable location. Stopping at the door to my office, I considered placing the photo on my computer desk, but realized Julianna could see it on her way to the bathroom. Besides, I was still casually browsing LDSsingles and didn't want a photo of Krista looking on when I used the site. Instead, I placed it on a shelf in the office closet and shut the door.

I felt good about my decision to move the photograph, but would it be enough? There were more photos of Krista in the house. Could I take them all down? What else would be required for Julianna to think I was ready to open my heart? I didn't have any answers, but told myself I would do whatever was needed.

•••

For the rest of the week, I worried Julianna would back out of our date. When my cell phone chirped, I hoped her number wouldn't appear on the screen. On the short drive to pick her up, I imagined her giving me a last-minute excuse. It wasn't until she opened the door that all my concerns vanished.

Julianna wore jeans and a white shirt that accentuated her slim, athletic build and hugged her body in the right places. Her long, curly hair hung past her shoulders. A Mona Lisa-like smile completed the package. My knees almost buckled at the sight, and I knew I couldn't let this beautiful woman slip through my fingers.

"You look gorgeous," I said.

Julianna's cheeks flushed. "Thanks," she replied.

I opened the car door for her, and we headed to a nearby barbeque restaurant. The plan was to get some food and drive to Antelope Island, a popular local attraction in the Great Salt Lake, where we could take in the scenery and get a close-up look at some buffalo.

Within minutes, I knew this date would be different. The tension and awkwardness that had existed between us on previous outings had vanished. Perhaps it was because Krista wasn't the proverbial elephant in the room or because Julianna thought we were simply going out as "friends." Whatever the reason, we clicked. We talked the entire drive to dinner and nonstop at the restaurant. The conversation flowed the way it would between two best friends who were catching up after not seeing each other in years.

As we got on the freeway, I cracked a joke, and the two of us burst into laughter. It was the deep laughter that makes your sides hurt, and it took all my concentration to keep the car on the road. When the laughter finally subsided, I glanced at Julianna at the exact moment she looked at me. For a split second, our eyes locked. A smile flashed across her face, her cheeks flushed, and she looked away. For several minutes, there was silence in the car, but it wasn't the uncomfortable kind that had filled our previous outings. It was the quiet and relaxed silence that occurs with people you know well, the kind where words aren't necessary. It was wonderful and frightening at the same time because it reminded me of the content, relaxed silence Krista and I had often shared.

Our conversation picked back up as we drove along the causeway to Antelope Island. The salty waters of the Great Salt Lake lapped at the road's rocky edges and seagulls glided in the sky, riding currents of hot summer air. On the island, we parked and took the short hike along Buffalo Point Trail. Then we drove along the island's east side, where we stopped to look at the buffalo that grazed near the road. We talked, joked, and laughed the entire time. It was quickly becoming one of the best dates I'd ever had.

As the sun dipped low, we started home. The road curved to the west, and crimson light enveloped the car. There was enough haze in the sky that you could look at the sun—a giant, red orb—for a brief second. The color of the sun and the sky was so vivid and spectacular that several other vehicles had pulled to the side of the road, and people stood outside their cars for a better look. I pulled over, and we both scrambled from the car. We stood side by side in silence and watched as the sun slowly set behind the Lakeside Mountains.

Before the sight vanished, I looked at Julianna and thought how gorgeous she looked bathed in scarlet. We stood close enough that I could have easily taken her hand in mine. Maybe if our previous dates had gone better, I would have done something, but I didn't want to risk ruining what had turned into a perfect evening together. Instead, I took a mental picture of her and turned my attention back to the sunset.

As we drove back over the causeway, Julianna said, "The sunset was amazing."

"A beautiful end to a beautiful day," I said.

We drove home in the same comfortable silence we had experienced earlier. Whenever I wanted to say something, I looked at Julianna. Our eyes never met, but each time, she had a content smile on her face, so I let the silence envelop the drive back to Ogden.

"I had a great evening," she said as we stopped in front of her door.

"Me too," I said.

"Will you be at church tomorrow?"

"Of course."

She smiled, and my heart thumped, thumped, thumped in my chest. I wanted to lean in and kiss her, but thought better of it. I didn't want to ruin what I considered a perfect date.

"See you tomorrow," she said before stepping into her apartment and shutting the door softly behind her.

I drove home at a leisurely pace because I didn't want the evening to end. I reasoned if I drove slowly enough, the night would last forever. I replayed the date over and over, and I hoped Julianna had enjoyed our time together as much as I had. Maybe this evening would be a turning point in our relationship.

At home, I readied for bed and opened the bedroom window to let in the night air and the sound of chirping crickets, hoping both would help me fall asleep. Lying in bed, my eyes drifted to Krista's graduation photo, and I realized that it was about a year ago we'd announced her pregnancy to family and friends. I remembered that instead of simply telling my family the good news, Krista had brought pickles and ice cream to a Sunday family dinner for dessert. When we served bowls of vanilla ice cream covered in dill pickles, everyone except my mom understood the message. She had looked at the food and then actually tried it, commenting on the odd flavor. My sister Bridget had rolled her eyes and said, "Mom, *it's pickles and ice cream! Pickles and ice cream!*" It took a moment for the message to click, but when it did, my mom burst into a huge smile, hugged Krista, and congratulated us on the news.

I smiled at the memory. It was the last time I remembered Krista being genuinely happy. Soon after that night, her mood and attitude darkened. I did the math and realized Hope would be seven months old if she had lived. What would Hope be like at that age? Could she sit up? Crawl? Suck her toes?

Anger at Krista dissolved my joy-filled evening. I turned on my side, my back to the photo, to stop fury and bitterness from overwhelming my mind. It didn't work. Images of Krista's dead body and Hope gasping her last breaths replaced the thoughts of Julianna and the picturesque red sunset. I closed my eyes and clenched my fists to force those images from my mind.

It took fifteen minutes and my remaining mental energy to clear my head. The anger, hate, and sorrow I felt were so powerful, they overwhelmed feelings of joy, love, and gratitude. I knew that if I couldn't resolve this conflict, these negative emotions would eventually destroy any future relationships. There had to be a way to get on top of them. I had tried exercise, meditation, and prayer, and the only result was that my rage occurred less frequently. It was progress, but not enough to make a relationship with Julianna succeed. I fell into a fitful sleep, not sure how to proceed.

PART TWO
Dating Life

CHAPTER SEVENTEEN

Julianna

After a fourteen-mile run, I lay in my usual spot in the middle of the trampoline, soaking up the sun. I had a Dean Koontz novel in one hand and a cold bottle of chocolate milk pressed against my side, but neither held my interest. Instead, I thought about Abel. After our wonderful trip to Antelope Island, we had gone out two more times. They were both perfect outings. And tonight we were going out again, a hike in the mountains east of Ogden.

Though I looked forward to our hike, I was anxious. I had volunteered to bring dinner, but I'd never made food for a guy I liked. What if Abel didn't enjoy it? I still didn't know how I felt about Krista and the afterlife. We had discussed her, his past, and their marriage on occasion as a natural part of getting to know each other better. There were still questions I needed to ask and something I needed to confess to Abel. I hoped to discuss these on our date if the moment presented itself, but

I worried that telling Abel more about myself would send the relationship into a tailspin.

All the "what ifs" made me glad any physical contact had been minimal. We had yet to kiss or hold hands. Sometimes we sat close enough that our arms brushed against each other or our legs touched. I sensed that Abel wanted to take things further, but refrained from making moves. I was grateful for the lack of physical affection because it made it easier to focus on whether Abel was ready to open his heart.

The sound of the lawn mower brought me out of my thoughts as my dad made a circle around the trampoline. He stopped the mower and pulled off the bag, sending the smell of freshly cut grass through the air.

"You haven't touched your drink," he said as he wiped his brow with the back of his arm. "Did the run take too much out of you?"

"I'm fine," I said. I moved to a sitting position and watched as he emptied the grass into a black plastic garbage bag. As he reattached the bag to the mower, I asked, "Can romantic feelings for someone change quickly?"

"What do you mean, Julie?"

I took a moment to choose my words carefully. "Can you care less about someone one day, and a few weeks later, have strong feelings for them?"

"I suppose so," he replied. "Did you have someone specific in mind?"

"Abel," I said, a little surprised how quickly his name came out of my mouth.

"Are you still seeing him? I thought you agreed to be friends."

"We've gone out a couple times since the friend talk," I confessed.

My dad raised his eyebrows and waited for me to continue.

"Dad, things have changed. They're good. Really, really good. I think about him all the time. We're going hiking this afternoon and I can't wait to see him again. If we keep going in this direction, I can see things getting very serious."

"That sounds like a good thing," my dad said.

"It is, and it isn't," I said. "Yes, I like spending time with him, but when I think of a future together . . ." My voice trailed off as I tried to compose my thoughts. "If he wasn't a widower, I'd be head over heels in love."

I waited for my dad to say something, but he didn't. I felt like he wanted more information, so I kept talking.

"Abel's not like Brian or any other guy I've gone out with," I said. "He makes sacrifices to spend time with me. When we're together, I feel like the center of his universe, but it also hurts me that he loves another woman. I don't like the idea of being number two. I want to be number one."

"Have you talked to Abel about this?"

I shook my head. "Not in-depth. I learned the basics of his marriage a few weeks ago. Since then, I've learned tidbits about Krista and their life together. I want to know more, but I'm afraid if I do, I'll compare myself to her and our relationship to their marriage. From what little I know, I already feel like I'll never measure up."

I looked at my dad for reassurance. I didn't know if my thoughts and feelings made any sense. I wanted someone to talk to—a family member or close family friend who had married or at least dated a widower who could impart some wisdom. But I didn't know anyone. Scouring the internet hadn't helped. I'd found a group called Second Wives Café, but the women on that site were dating or married to divorced men.

Finally, my dad spoke. "This isn't something I have experience with. Have you prayed about it?"

I didn't want to pray about it. I wanted my dad to impart some of his valuable relationship wisdom and insights. My gut told me Dad was right, but what if I prayed and received an answer I didn't want or like? What if God told me to be okay with being number two? Did I have the faith to accept that answer? I didn't know.

"Sort of," I said.

"Sort of? What does that mean?"

"It means I haven't prayed seriously about it," I admitted.

"I wish I had the answers to your concerns," my dad said. "But you know how to get answers and direction."

My dad started the mower, and I laid back on the trampoline. Thirty thousand feet above, a jet left puffy white contrails as it streaked across the sky. My dad was right. I knew what to do, but didn't know if I had the courage to do it.

•••

Abel picked me up late in the afternoon. We drove to North Ogden Divide, where several trailheads converged. On the way, he told me the plan was to hike toward Lewis Peak and find a private spot to eat dinner. Because Abel was excited about the hike, I didn't tell him about my fourteen-mile run earlier that morning. Every muscle in my legs ached as we hiked the steep trail. After two miles, the trail flattened and we stopped on a rocky ledge that overlooked Ogden Valley to the east. We were both soaked with sweat and decided this would be a good location to rest and eat. We sat on a rock ledge, drank cold water, and dangled our feet over the side. I took in the rural green valley below. Most of the houses were big and had five- or ten-acre yards. In the distance, the road that made up the first third of the Ogden Marathon snaked into the valley. Below, a construction crew framed a new home, and a group of seven kids played tag in a neighboring backyard.

"It's beautiful up here," I said.

"I love this view." Abel had a distant look on his face, and I wondered what, or who, he was thinking about. I considered asking, but decided against it. There would be time for that later.

My stomach rumbled. "Want some food?" I said, opening my backpack.

"Yeah, I'm starving," Abel said.

We ate the turkey sandwiches, carrot sticks, chips, and homemade cookies in silence. In the valley below, I watched the group of kids run around their two-acre yard and thought it would be nice to have a big yard where my future children could play with each other. At some point, I glanced at Abel and caught him taking a long look at me. He smiled then glanced away, perhaps slightly embarrassed I had caught him.

"What are you looking at?" I asked.

"You," Abel replied.

"Why me?"

"Because you're beautiful."

A wave of heat washed over me. I looked away, unsure how to handle the compliment.

"I'm just plain and ordinary," I said.

"No, you're not," Abel said, inching closer to me.

"How do you know that?"

"Because I don't go out with plain and ordinary women."

A bead of sweat ran down my face. I wiped it away with the back of my hand and kept my eyes locked on the valley below. A large white cooler rested on the tailgate of a truck, and the construction crew stood in a half circle taking long drinks from silver aluminum cans. Abel had given me a great compliment and under any other circumstances I would have inched closer to him or leaned my head on his shoulder, but I couldn't bring myself to do it—not with so many unanswered questions about what our eternal future would look like. Instead, I did the only thing I could think of to flirt back—I locked eyes with Abel and smiled.

"How is it a beautiful woman like you doesn't have guys asking her out all the time?" Abel said.

"Who said I don't?"

Abel opened his mouth to say something, but closed it. He removed his baseball hat and wiped the sweat off his forehead with the back of his arm.

"Are you dating other guys?" he said, his tone less playful and confident.

"Yes," I said. "Well, I was until a couple of weeks ago."

"What happened a couple of weeks ago?"

"I broke it off."

"You had a boyfriend?" Abel said.

"Sort of. We weren't exclusive. That's why I went out with you." I took a drink from my water bottle. "You seem surprised."

Abel took a bite of his sandwich and swallowed before speaking. "Is it officially over between you and this guy?"

I nodded. "I broke up with him the same day we had the 'friend' talk."

"Why'd you end it with him?"

"Lots of reasons. Distance was one. He lives in Provo. It made it hard to see each other regularly. I need to spend time with someone if I'm going to be in a serious relationship. Weekly visits and daily phone calls aren't enough."

Abel stared at something in the valley below, his face expressionless. I took another drink of water before continuing.

"We might have overcome the distance issue if we both put more effort into seeing each other, but he was okay with occasional visits, and I got tired of doing all the heavy lifting."

"That explains why I never saw him at church," Abel said.

"Would you have asked me out if he came with me?"

Abel let out a long breath, ran his hands through his hair, and put his hat back on before answering. "I don't know. It took months to find the courage to talk to you. If I had seen you with someone else, I'd probably still be watching from a distance."

I looked back over the valley and wondered how different my life would be if Brian had attended church with me once. Would I be on the mountain talking to Abel now? It made me realize how sometimes small, seemingly insignificant choices can have enormous consequences.

"Since we're discussing dating," Abel said, "there's a question I've been wanting to ask. Why did you go out with me again after our awful first date?"

"So, you agree our first date was terrible?"

"One of the worst."

"You really want to know?"

"I do."

I took a deep breath before answering.

"My dad suggested I give you a second chance."

"Really?" Abel said.

"He thought it was your first date since your wife died and you were out of practice."

Abel chucked. "I'll have to thank him when I meet him."

Meet him? Was Abel already thinking about meeting my family? I needed answers to my questions before that could happen. But since we were on the topic, this seemed like a good chance to ask some questions that were on my mind.

"Was I your first date?" I said. "I mean, since Krista died."

I hoped the answer was no. Though I couldn't explain why, I didn't want to be the first and only woman Abel had gone out with since becoming widowed.

"I've dated off and on since April," he said.

"Were any of them as awful as our first date?"

Abel chuckled. "No, but most of them had awkward moments. Dating is different when you're a widower."

We finished our dinner in silence. The wind picked up, and I brushed my hair from my eyes. Questions about Krista swirled through my mind. Should I ask them? Worried about ruining another wonderful evening, I said nothing. When we started talking, the conversation shifted to other topics. The shadows grew long. Abel took a long drink from his water bottle and stood and stretched.

"We should get going if we want to get back to the car before dark," he said.

Instead of getting up, I stared out at the valley below. The kids who had played outside the entire time we talked ran into the house in one giant horde as if they were called in for dinner. The construction workers packed up their tools and loaded up their trucks. This was an opportune time to ask Abel the questions that weighed on my mind. I hoped my curiosity wouldn't set our relationship back.

"Everything okay?" Abel said.

"I have some questions about Krista," I said.

Abel stood for a long moment before sitting back on the ledge.

"Sure," he said. "What do you want to know?"

I took a deep breath and asked, "Do you know why she killed herself?"

Abel's body stiffened.

"No," he said after a moment. "I don't know why she did it."

"Did she leave a note?"

"No."

"Were there signs she was suicidal?"

Abel let out a slow sigh. He took off his baseball hat and twirled it on his fingers before putting it back on his head.

"Krista was vivacious and outgoing," he said. "She could light up a room just by walking into it. After talking to her for a few minutes, you felt like her best friend. Everyone wanted to be around her. That was the woman I fell in love with."

Even though Abel wasn't comparing the two of us, that was where my mind went. Outgoing. Life of the party. Personable. Was that the type of woman Abel liked? Personality wise, Krista and I were opposites. What did he see in me? How could I ever measure up?

"The last two months of her life, Krista completely changed," Abel continued. "The woman who was so excited to start a family and be a mom—"

Abel's voice caught. I bit my lower lip, wondering if I had pushed the subject too far. I let the silence hang, unsure what to say or do if Abel started crying. But the tears didn't fall. Abel swallowed hard before continuing.

"As her pregnancy progressed, her personality changed. She didn't want to spend time with anyone. She would cancel planned activities with friends at the last minute. About a month before she died, she quit her job without giving notice. Toward the end, she wouldn't get dressed or ready for the day. Her mood darkened, and she became more despondent. She was the complete opposite of the woman I married. Looking back, I should have been more concerned, but I never thought she would hurt herself or our baby."

Somewhere behind us, the cheerful voices of hikers grew louder, then faded away, and the calm silence of the mountains returned. I waited for Abel to continue, but his eyes remained focused on something across the valley. Physically, he was next to me, but his mind was somewhere far away and distant—another lifetime away.

Finally, I asked, "Did Krista suffer from depression?"

Abel shrugged. "Maybe. An undiagnosed mental illness might have played a part too. I've racked my brain and searched the internet for answers, but I don't know what made her suicidal. I'm trying to make peace with the fact that I may never know why she did it. At least not in this life, anyway."

As the gravity of Abel's words sank in, I debated what to say next. I needed to tell him something, but didn't know the best way to bring it up.

"Why all the questions?" Abel said. "It's not the most uplifting topic."

I swallowed hard before answering. This was what I needed him to know. "Because I have depression. It's something I've struggled with for ten years."

Abel's expression remained blank.

"Oh," he said. Then, "How bad is it?"

"I'm not suicidal, if that's what you're asking," I said. "I've never thought about taking my own life, but since you lost your wife to suicide, I thought you needed to know."

"What are you doing to treat it?" Abel asked.

"Medication. Running. Serving others. Prayer. It depends on how things are going. Right now, I'm not taking medication, but that could change."

Abel nodded. "I like how you're being proactive about tackling the problem."

"I try to stay ahead of it. People have more control over their bodies and emotions than they think. Sometimes medication is necessary, but not always. That's one reason I run. Serving others keeps me in a good place mentally. So does prayer. If I'm not doing those things, I struggle."

"Thanks for letting me know," Abel said.

I waited for the other shoe to drop, for Abel to say something about having to think things over or he couldn't date someone who had depression. Instead, he stood and put on his backpack. "It's getting dark. We should go."

As we started down the mountain, the sun, large and orange like a basketball, began its journey below the horizon. I calculated there was barely enough light for us to make it back to his car before it got dark. We hiked in silence. I worried what Abel was thinking and if he was having second thoughts about a relationship. He appeared fine, but maybe that would change once he had time to think things over.

Near the trailhead, Abel stopped and picked some wildflowers near the edge of the trail. With a slight bow, he handed them to me.

"For you, my lady," he said, smiling.

As I took the flowers, our eyes met, and an unspoken message passed between us. I knew my depression wasn't an issue with Abel. There was something in the smile on his face and the way he bowed as he handed me the flowers that erased my worry. A feeling of peace and relief filled my heart.

After Abel dropped me off, I showered and got ready for bed. I was physically exhausted and wanted to fall right to sleep. As I pulled back the covers, I felt prompted to get on my knees and pray about Abel.

I had prayed about a relationship with him before, but tonight it wasn't my normal prayer. This time I told Heavenly Father everything—my concerns about getting serious with a young widower, my worries about his previous sealing to Krista, and how things would work out with the three of us in the next life. I told Him I didn't think I could measure up to Krista and confessed my insecurities about feeling like a consolation prize. I prayed long and hard, then stayed on my knees waiting for an answer.

Stories about people getting immediate and sometimes dramatic answers to prayers fill Latter-day Saint scripture and culture. Countless times in church, couples share stories about praying to know whether they should marry the person they were dating and receiving powerful, quick confirmations. I hoped to receive a similar answer, but nothing came. There was no feeling of peace or reassurance, no words of comfort or other signs that I should marry or keep dating Abel. This was not what I had expected. For a long time, I remained on my knees, hoping for an answer, but for whatever reason, the heavens remained closed.

CHAPTER EIGHTEEN

Abel

The day after our hike, I awoke to a sunlight-drenched room and the screeching of magpies in the black walnut tree next to my home. I took a moment to enjoy the cool morning air blowing through the open window. My legs were stiff from the hike, but I shrugged off the discomfort. Sore muscles were a small price to pay for a memorable evening with Julianna.

My mind drifted to the future. I could envision marrying Julianna, having a family together, and spending the rest of my life—and eternity—with her. The strong attraction I initially felt was still there, but combined with thoughts of an eternal relationship, it had turned into something richer and deeper. They were the same feelings I felt for Krista. This was an exhilarating and scary realization. I hadn't thought it was possible to have the same love for two very different people. I often heard parents say they had the same love for their children no matter how many or how different their children were. Could one feel the same way about living and deceased spouses?

My bigger concern was whether my love for Julianna was genuine. It felt real, but how could I be sure? I didn't want to marry someone for the wrong reasons. Whether I married Julianna or someone else, I wanted it to be because I truly loved and cared about her—not because I needed to fill the hole Krista had left in my heart and my life.

With these thoughts on my mind, I got out of bed and made breakfast. I'd just finished flipping the last pancake when my mom knocked on the door. She had a smile on her face and a large book in her right hand.

"I made something for you," she said, holding the book up for me to see.

It was a scrapbook. Pink, green, and yellow fabric made up the soft cover. There was a large brown teddy bear in the center. Instinctively I knew which photos it held. The cool morning air turned hot, and it felt like someone had just dropped fifty-pound weights on my shoulders.

"What's this?" I asked.

"I put together photographs of Hope for you," my mom said, confirming my suspicions.

I stared at the scrapbook for a long moment before taking it. Tears bubbled in the corners of my eyes, and it took all of my mental fortitude to keep them at bay.

"Thanks," I said. "That means a lot to me."

"Do you want to look at it?" my mom said.

From the way she asked, I knew my mom wanted to look at the scrapbook together. Looking at the cover alone, it was obvious she had put a lot of time into the project and was proud of her work. But I couldn't look at the contents. Though I was making good progress when it came to Krista-related grief, I hadn't started working on my sorrow and anguish for Hope. Thoughts of her brought instant tears to my eyes, but also intense rage and hatred for Krista. The unresolved grief and raw emotions were the reasons why there were no photos of my daughter in my home. The morning had started off so nice, and dealing with these emotions was the last thing I wanted to do.

"Maybe later," I said. "There are other things I need to take care of this morning."

"Are you sure?"

"Mom, please. Not now," I replied.

If my mom took offense, she didn't show it. Thankfully, she didn't press the issue further.

After she left, I held the scrapbook in my hands, debating what to do with it. My emotional side wanted to throw it in the trash, but my logical side knew I'd eventually regret that decision. Curious what it contained, I opened it to a random page. My eyes went straight to a photo of me holding Hope. Because she was connected to so many machines, holding her required the help of a nurse, and was something I only did a handful of times. My daughter looked small and helpless in my arms, and the picture blurred from the tears. A tsunami of dormant Hope memories washed over me. I snapped the scrapbook shut and tossed it on the coffee table. Maybe one day I'd be able to look through the photos without crying, but not today. Or maybe that day would never come.

•••

Because of a family event, Julianna attended church in Taylorsville. After the emotions of that morning, her absence turned out to be for the best. Arriving at church, I was uptight, angry, and on the verge of tears. It took the entire three hours of worship services and classes to reset my emotions. By the time Julianna arrived at my house for dinner, I felt like my normal self.

I don't remember what we made, but I remember everything felt natural as we worked together in the kitchen preparing the meal. As we ate, laughed, and enjoyed the food, spending the rest of our lives together seemed like a reality instead of fantasy. After we cleaned up, we moved to the living room, where the conversation and laughter continued. Things were going so well, I thought this might be a good time to share our first kiss.

I sat close enough to Julianna on the couch that our legs and hips touched. When she didn't scoot away, I took this as a sign that she wouldn't rebuff my efforts to kiss her.

"What's this?" Julianna said, pointing to Hope's scrapbook on the coffee table.

A cold chill replaced the excitement and happiness that permeated the evening. I cursed myself under my breath for not putting the book elsewhere. I didn't want to talk about Hope.

"Photos of my daughter," I said, hoping my voice wouldn't crack when I spoke. "It's something my mom put together."

Julianna leaned forward and traced the edge of the scrapbook with her finger. "Can I look at it?"

I swallowed hard before answering. I didn't care if Julianna looked at the photos. At some point, she would need to learn more about my daughter and her brief life. The problem was that I didn't know if I could keep my emotions in check. Glancing at one photograph that morning had turned me into an emotional mess. How would I react looking through its entire contents? Things were going so well between the two of us, I didn't want Julianna thinking I wasn't ready to move forward. I did a quick check and thought I could stomach my way through it.

"Of course," I said. "You can look at it."

Julianna placed the scrapbook on her lap and opened the cover. The first page contained a single photo of Hope lying in the incubator where she had spent most of her life. A tube from a ventilator snaked its way across her face and down her throat. Tiny electrodes spotted her chest, arms, and legs. Somehow the nurses found room to connect an IV. I had forgotten how much medical equipment it took to keep her alive, and the photo reminded me of something from a dystopian movie. Grief bubbled up to the surface, and I glanced down at the floor.

You can do this, Abel, I thought. *Take a deep breath and push through this.*

"Look at all the hair on her head," Julianna said. Then, "How early was she born?"

"Two months."

"How big was she?"

"Eighteen inches," I said.

"How much did she weigh?"

"Just over two pounds."

Julianna turned another page. I kept my eyes focused on the floor. After a moment she said, "Was she at Primary Children's?"

Located in Salt Lake, Primary Children's Medical Center is the top pediatric hospital in the Intermountain West.

"Yes," I replied.

I heard another page turn. I glanced at the photos. Some were of Hope. Others were of friends and family paying her a visit. I looked away.

"How long did she live?"

"Nine days."

"She's beautiful," Julianna said.

"Thanks."

As Julianna worked her way through the scrapbook, I peeked at enough photos to see that my mom had divided its contents into three sections. The first contained photos of Hope in the hospital, along with me, and others who came to visit. The second part, the shortest of the three, chronicled the day I removed her from life support. Her funeral filled the final section.

Julianna looked at every photo. She asked about the people she didn't know and had questions about Hope's medical conditions. Sometimes I looked at the photos along with her. Other times, I focused on the far wall or the carpet, blinking quickly to fight away the tears.

"Why did you remove her from life support?" Julianna asked as we reached the second section of the album.

I glanced at the scrapbook. In the photos, I sat in an armchair holding Hope, surrounded by immediate family and a few close friends. It took close to two hours for Hope to take her last breath. During that time, everyone said their goodbyes and left. At the end, it was only my dad and I. The memories of that day were too fresh, and I could only look at the pictures for a few seconds before looking away.

"Brain damage," I said. "The doctors said she didn't get enough oxygen between Krista's death and her delivery. Scans showed massive amounts of blood on her brain." My mind flashed back to the black and white images of Hope's head and seeing large dark spots on both hemispheres of her brain. I recalled the sense of defeat and hopelessness that accompanied the diagnosis.

"I thought her condition would improve after a few days," I continued, "but it became apparent she could only survive with the help of machines. That didn't seem like much of a life, so I decided to—"

My voice cracked as memories of holding Hope as she took her last breaths rushed through my mind. I wiped a tear from my eye with the back of my hand, sadness crashing through the mental blocks I had hastily erected.

Julianna focused her attention on the scrapbook—or so it seemed. Maybe she was being polite. She took her time looking at the last several pages, which contained photographs of Hope's funeral. We sat in silence, and I used the time to regain control of my emotions.

"That must have been hard," Julianna said as she closed the scrapbook. "I can't imagine what it would be like to lose a child."

"I hope it's something you never have to experience," I said.

"Are these the only photos of her?"

I shook my head. "I took some too. They're in a box somewhere."

Things were quiet between us for the space of three breaths, then Julianna said, "You don't have any photographs of her on the walls."

I nodded.

"Why?"

"They're too painful to look at."

"Oh," Julianna said. She looked at the scrapbook on her lap as if it were a snake.

"I'm glad we went through it," I said, putting my hand on her knee. "I needed to look through it sooner or later. Better to do it with you than alone."

In the quiet that followed, I debated where to take the conversation. I needed to tell Julianna something, but I was unsure if this was the time to do it. I had considered telling her last night after she told me about her depression, but the mood had gone from serious to light quickly, and it didn't feel like the right time. Now the atmosphere was heavy and thick. What I needed to tell her would only add to it. I might as well get it over with.

"It's my fault Krista died," I said.

"What do you mean?" Julianna said, her brow furrowed.

I took a moment to compose my thoughts. What I was about to tell Julianna, I had confessed to only one other person.

"I ignored three promptings that might have saved Krista's life," I said.

Julianna scooted a few inches away. I couldn't tell if she wanted to look me in the eyes or if she didn't want to sit close anymore. I kept talking.

"The night before Krista killed herself, I came home from work to an empty apartment. Krista had left a note saying she wanted to spend the night at her grandmother's house. I felt angry and upset at her decision because of my exhausting day at work. I wanted to relax, not drive to Ogden. Anyway, I packed an overnight bag and put it in my trunk. As I was about to drive away, I had the distinct impression I should go back to the apartment, get my gun, and give it to my brother for safekeeping."

I took a moment, reliving the memory before continuing.

"I shrugged off the feeling and drove to her grandmother's house, where we spent the night. I got up early to run some errands. My plan was to get them done quickly so Krista and I could spend the day together. As I backed out of the driveway, I had a strong feeling that instead of going to the store, I should return to the apartment. But I didn't want to go back. We had just moved into the apartment and we needed some supplies, so I pushed the feeling to the side and started checking things off my list."

I gathered my thoughts and gave Julianna a chance to say something. She remained silent. A mix of worry, concern, and compassion crossed her face. At least, that was how I interpreted it. It reminded me that despite my intense feelings, I didn't know her well enough to be certain. I let out a slow breath and continued the rest of the story.

"When I returned to her grandmother's house a couple of hours later, Krista was gone. I called the apartment and asked why she'd left. Krista kept telling me she just needed a few things and would be coming back soon, but after a couple hours of this, it became apparent that she wasn't really going to return. After some choice words, I drove to the apartment. Her car was parked in front, but the apartment itself was dark and the curtains drawn. At that moment, I realized something was seriously wrong. I felt strongly that I should open the door quietly and enter the apartment without saying a word, but I was so uptight and worried that I brushed aside that prompting too. I hurried inside, called out her name, and a moment later, I heard a gunshot."

Things were quiet between Julianna and I for only a few seconds, but those moments felt like an eternity. Latter-day Saint history contains countless stories of pioneers, prophets, and ordinary women and men who followed spiritual impressions. Obeying these feelings often resulted in miracles. One story I had heard many times was when Wilford Woodruff, one of the nineteenth-century prophets of the Church, slept outside in his wagon with his wife and child. In the middle of the night, he felt prompted to move his wagon. Instead of dismissing this idea, he obeyed. Soon after, a storm arose and uprooted a tree that landed in the exact spot where his wagon had been. Most stories weren't that dramatic, but they all demonstrated that following promptings, no matter how small or insignificant, always led to positive outcomes. Rarely were stories told about people who ignored those feelings and the negative consequences of their decisions.

For me, the results of ignoring these promptings were twofold—I felt responsible for Krista and Hope's death, and I felt unworthy of God's love. I had often felt that a just punishment for my inaction would be to spend the rest of my life alone, sad, and miserable—never to fall in love again. As the seconds dragged by, I thought that if Julianna wanted nothing more to do with me, I'd let her go. If she walked out of my life, I would completely understand, and that might even help me feel that heavenly justice had been served.

Julianna set the scrapbook on the coffee table. "That must be hard to live with," she said.

"I'm still trying to forgive myself," I said.

I waited for Julianna to get up from the couch and make an excuse about needing to leave, but she didn't. We switched topics, and the evening continued. I can't remember what we talked about, but we kept the conversation light. To my surprise, Julianna invited me to her place for dinner after work the next evening. Still, as I walked her to her car, any desire to kiss her had vanished. As I watched Julianna drive away, I wondered if grief and guilt would stop me from opening my heart, and if this relationship could ever turn into something serious and wonderful.

CHAPTER NINETEEN

Julianna

As someone who struggled with depression, it was hard not to take Krista's suicide personally. There had been a handful of times where I had struggled with similar feelings but had always managed to pull myself back from the brink. What usually saved me was knowing how taking my own life would hurt my family, friends, and other loved ones. How had Krista not foreseen the pain and devastation her actions would cause?

Since I knew so little about Krista or the circumstances surrounding her death, I tried not to judge her. However, that became more difficult after looking through Hope's scrapbook. Seeing Abel's sad face and the images of his helpless premature daughter had brought out intense feelings of anger. What kind of woman would consider taking her own life when she was pregnant? Did she even love Abel or her unborn child? The photo of Abel carrying Hope's small white casket to the gravesite, the visceral pain and sorrow on his face, stoked my rage until it filled my body. I didn't enjoy these feelings, but was unsure how to handle such intense emotions or even if I should mention them to Abel. Instead, I let them smolder, knowing that they would need to be confronted in the future.

Abel's confession about ignoring spiritual promptings had also surprised me. I had always done my best to listen to spiritual guidance and was still trying to receive answers to my own prayers about Abel, but I also reflected on past mistakes I had made. Though they seemed small compared to Abel's missteps, there were past decisions I wished I could take back. What if I had ignored a serious prompting or a warning? How would I want Abel to respond? I knew I would hope my slip-ups would be treated with compassion and understanding—just like he had responded to my confession about depression. I needed to treat Abel in the same manner I wanted to be treated. From the pained look on his face and his struggle to keep his emotions in check as he told me Hope's story, he appeared to be in a lot of anguish over his inaction. I thought the best way forward was to let him work through his issues while I worked on my own concerns.

That night, I got on my knees and poured out my soul in prayer about Abel. I asked Heavenly Father whether I should continue dating him, if I should marry him—and, if we were to get married, what would our relationship look like in the eternities. I also prayed that I would stop feeling angry at Krista and try to better understand her actions. Once again, the heavens remained silent.

As I got into bed, I wondered if an answer would ever come. I knew that there were times when the Lord expected me to make my own decisions. However, these were not trivial concerns. Marrying Abel had eternal consequences, and I didn't want to consider marriage or a serious relationship without some heavenly guidance or direction. I told my dad about my lack of answers and asked him for suggestions on how to proceed.

"Until an answer comes, spend as much time with Abel as possible," my dad said. "That should give you a good idea if he's ready for a serious relationship."

"We already spend most evenings together," I said. "Same with the weekends. The only time we're apart is during work or my training runs."

"What do you do when you're together?"

"Make dinner, buy groceries, talk, hike, read."

"That's a good way to spend your time. Do you think he's ready to open his heart?"

I shrugged. "It's obvious he has strong feelings for me, but he's also still grieving. I'm just trying to figure out how to know where he's at in the process."

"What about asking him to run with you?"

Inviting Abel on my training runs was something I had considered for the last two weeks but worried the distance and speed would be too much for him.

"I know he'd say yes," I said. "He's thrown around hints that he'd like to run with me."

"Why don't you ask him?"

"I'm worried he won't stick with it. I run farther, faster, and harder than him. The other guys who've run with me gave up after two or three runs. I don't want running to strain our relationship."

"Julie," my dad said, "if he's ready to move forward, he won't let something like running get in the way."

I thought about what my dad had said. Would my training schedule be too much for Abel? There was only one way to find out.

•••

The morning of our first run together, Abel knocked at my door at five a.m., dressed in running clothes and an ear-to-ear smile. Prompt and happy. I took that as a good sign.

"How far are we running today?" he asked.

"Eight miles."

Abel nodded. "Sounds good."

"It's a pace run," I said.

"Okay. How fast?"

"Six-thirty miles."

Abel paused. "Six minutes and thirty seconds?"

Though I didn't know it, Abel had never run so far or fast before. Had I known this, I would have started him on a less strenuous run.

"Yes, I need to keep that pace. I can't slow down," I said.

"I'll do my best to keep up," Abel said.

I outlined the course for Abel, and we started running. For the first two miles, Abel matched me stride for stride, but soon, I inched ahead. When he disappeared from my peripheral vision, I didn't look back.

At the four-mile mark, I turned around to retrace the route home and saw Abel in the morning's blue-gray light a half mile behind. He waved, smiled, and turned around as I flew past him. After completing the run, I waited at the entrance of the apartment complex. As the minutes ticked by, I worried I had pushed him too far and too fast. Would he want to run with me again? Ten minutes later, Abel finished, his shirt soaked with sweat and his face beet red.

"You're fast," he said between breaths.

He accepted my invitation for a drink of water and hurried home to get ready for work. After he left, I wondered if he would show up the next morning.

But I shouldn't have. At exactly five a.m., Abel knocked on my door. He wore different running clothes, but still had a big, bright smile. Our second run was shorter and slower, and once again, I pulled ahead after two miles and waited for Abel to finish. This routine continued for the next several weeks and at some point, I stopped worrying whether Abel would quit. His speed and stamina increased. After completing longer runs of six or more miles, instead of waiting several minutes for him to finish, he was only a minute behind. On runs under six miles, he was often right on my heels.

Soon, our morning runs became more than marathon training. They became our thing—something that only the two of us shared. Each run created and strengthened a bond between us even though not a single word was spoken. I looked forward to the knock on my door each morning and seeing Abel ready to tackle whichever run my training schedule demanded. We would drink cold glasses of water after our runs and plan our evenings. Some nights, we decided we'd run errands or eat dinner together. Other nights, we were too physically exhausted to do more than sit on the couch and talk or watch a mindless crime drama on television. On those too-tired-to-do-anything evenings, we'd hold hands and rest our heads on the shoulder or arm of the other person.

It took time to reach that level of physical comfort. We started by sitting close enough that the sides of our arms and legs would touch. That led to handholding, then being comfortable enough to rest hands on the legs of the other. Abel would later describe it like being "two awkward teenagers" who were figuring out their first relationship. With all our unanswered questions and concerns, I was grateful that this part of our relationship progressed slowly.

As much as I enjoyed Abel's arms around me and resting my head on his shoulder, I drew the line at kissing. I didn't have a lot of experience in the kissing department. I knew that Abel wanted to take that step but I wasn't ready. I didn't want to become more attached until I had some heavenly guidance and direction.

It was during one of these evenings together that I discovered Abel still wore his wedding band. We'd cleaned up dinner and turned on some reality show on TV. Too tired to give it much attention, I rested my head on his shoulder and put my hand on his chest. I closed my eyes and ran the tips of my fingers up and down his breastbone until I felt something round and hard under his shirt.

"What's this?" I said, raising my head.

"Oh, it's my wedding band," Abel said nonchalantly. He reached under his T-shirt and pulled out a domed gold band attached to a chain around his neck. Before I could get a look at it, he had stuffed it back in his shirt.

A sour feeling started in my stomach and rose to my throat. I swallowed hard to push it down. I had seen the chain around Abel's neck, but I didn't know about the band. If I had known Abel wore his wedding ring, I wouldn't have allowed things to become so serious between the two of us. Should I say something about it and ask him to remove it? What was the best way to even broach the topic? The moment was another stinging reminder that this relationship didn't have a road map. Abel settled back into the couch, seemingly indifferent to the magnitude of the revelation. I leaned against him, but not as close as before, and kept my hands in my lap. While the show continued, I remained lost in my thoughts.

"I should go," Abel said when the show ended.

Instead of standing up and putting his shoes on, he rested his head on mine—a sign that he wanted to stay and talk. But I didn't want him to stay. I needed some time alone to figure out what to do next. I stood, picked up the two empty water glasses from the floor, and put them in the dishwasher. I wiped down the already clean counters, hoping Abel understood I wasn't returning to the couch. After a minute, Abel got the message. He stood, walked to the door, and slipped on his shoes without tying them. I tossed the rag in the sink and stood six feet from Abel, my arms folded.

"We running tomorrow morning?" he asked.

"Yes," I said despite feeling like I never wanted to run with Abel ever again. How could he want to spend each morning together or think about kissing me while wearing a symbol of commitment to Krista? I wasn't a mistress, but after discovering his wedding band, I sure felt like one.

Abel's body swayed ever so slightly in my direction, inviting me closer. I kept my eyes locked on the small bump under his T-shirt.

"See you tomorrow," I said, trying to put just enough firmness in my voice to convey that this was goodnight.

It must have worked because Abel said, "Five a.m.," before leaving.

I let out a breath and locked the door. As I readied for bed, my mind raced. Was the ring a sign that Abel couldn't love me? Perhaps my prayers remained unanswered because God had wanted me to find the ring and figure it out on my own.

That night, I couldn't sleep. I tossed and turned, trying to wrap my mind around the wedding band. We needed to talk about it, but how did I bring it up without upsetting Abel? Would asking him to take it off end our relationship just as it was blossoming? What would I do if Abel refused to remove it? By the time I fell into a fitful sleep, I didn't have any answers, and no idea what I was going to do about it.

CHAPTER TWENTY

Abel

I was in love with Julianna. Whenever we spent time together, I wanted to take her in my arms and let her know how much she meant to me. But each time the words "I love you" bubbled up my throat, I pushed them back down. I worried those three words would scare her away. Our relationship often felt like it was one widower-related issue from imploding. Julianna knew I still loved Krista. How would she react knowing that part of my heart was reserved for another woman? Not having an answer, I held my tongue, but repeated "I love you" over and over in my mind whenever we were together.

My inability to tell Julianna how I felt about her highlighted my struggle to find a balance between honoring my life and marriage to Krista and focusing on building a new one. These two parts of my life couldn't coexist, which made it impossible to love Julianna and Krista at the same time. If, for example, I remembered Krista, her death, and the life we shared, my love for Julianna diminished. Conversely, if I focused my thoughts and attention on Julianna, my life with Krista seemed more like a distant but pleasant memory.

This conflict, which occurred multiple times every day, reminded me of Jesus's Sermon on the Mount, where He taught that a person couldn't serve two masters. In my case, who did I want to prioritize in my life—Krista or Julianna? Truthfully, I didn't want to pick. I wanted to figure out a solution where I could balance my love for Krista and my growing feelings for Julianna. But the more time I spent with Julianna, the more I realized such a compromise was impossible. I needed to decide who would get the lion's share of my heart.

This struggle manifested itself over dinner one evening. Julianna had made spaghetti, garlic bread, and a salad. We ate at her small table in silence, both hungry from all the mileage we'd run that week. As I pushed my empty plate to the side, Julianna asked how I enjoyed living so close to my parents.

"It wouldn't be my first choice," I said.

"Why do you live there?"

"My wife . . . I mean, Krista, wanted to buy the house. She wanted to fix it up so we could live close to her family and mine."

My wife. The two words felt clunky. I usually referred to Krista as "my wife," but tonight, in the presence of someone I hoped to marry one day, they didn't feel right. I didn't know if Julianna picked up on the fact that I had stumbled over those words or if it was something she wanted to talk about, but she put down her fork and leaned forward.

"I don't mind that Krista comes up in conversation," she said. "But when you refer to her as 'my wife,' it makes me feel like you're not ready to open your heart. I can only be with you if I know you're ready to start a new life with me."

Julianna spoke so confidently, I thought she wanted to end the relationship. Years later, I learned she was terrified her comment would upset me. Instead, I went into overdrive, trying to figure out a better way to refer to Krista. Dead or deceased wife? That sounded creepy. My wife in heaven? No, that sounded even more awkward. First wife? Better, but not the best solution.

Unable to come up with a replacement, I said, "How would you like me to refer to her?"

Julianna shrugged. "I don't know. I can't think of anything."

"I don't have an answer either."

"We don't have to solve this issue now," Julianna said. "I'm just letting you know that when you refer to Krista as 'my wife,' it makes me feel that you're not ready to move forward."

I drummed my fingers on the table and tried to see things from her point of view. The phrase "my wife" was an active, living way of referring to Krista. It showed she had priority in my life and in my heart. How would I feel if I was dating a widow who constantly referred to her deceased spouse as "my husband"? The words "diminished" and "placeholder" came to mind.

"Give me some time to think it over," I said.

We switched topics and finished dinner, though I don't know how present I was the rest of the evening. My mind kept drifting back to a better way to refer to Krista without making Julianna feel like second best.

I returned home full, but frustrated. Every time things went well with Julianna, another widower-related issue stalled our progress. In the hall, I stopped and examined our engagement photo. Krista had loved the picture and hung it prominently on the walls of the various places we lived. I liked it because Krista looked so happy. Happy. That was how I liked to remember her.

Twice, I had noticed Julianna giving the photo a passing glance as she went down the hall to the bathroom. I thought little of it at the time, but tonight I wondered how she felt whenever she saw the photos. She had spoken up about referring to Krista as "my wife," but had said nothing about the photos. Did that mean they didn't bother her, or that she didn't know how to discuss them? With our dinner conversation weighing heavily on my mind, I leaned toward the latter and wondered if photos of Krista also made Julianna feel like she was dating a married man. What did widows and widowers do with photographs of their deceased spouses after they became serious with someone else? Keep one or two up? Combine them with photos of their new love? Take them all down? I didn't know. Once again, I had to figure things out on my own.

I thought things over as I readied for bed. When I finished brushing my teeth, I returned to the engagement photo and took it down. I was curious if Julianna would notice and say something, but I also wanted to see how removing it would affect me. Would it make it easier to focus on Julianna if there were fewer reminders of Krista in my house? There was only one way to find out.

I placed the photo in my office closet next to the one I had removed from the table.

"I love you, Krista," I said before closing the door.

•••

A possible solution to how to refer to Krista came to me in the middle of our run the following morning. I wanted to tell

Julianna to stop running so I could explain my solution. Instead, I waited until after the run to share the news.

As we walked back to her apartment, sweat dripping down our faces, I said. "I thought of a way to refer to Krista."

Julianna gave me an expectant look.

"What if I referred to her as my 'late wife' or simply 'Krista'?"

Julianna nodded her head but said nothing. She didn't speak until we reached the door of her apartment.

"I think that will work," she said. "Let's try it and see how it goes."

I glanced at my watch. The run had gone on longer than planned, and I had to hurry home and clean up if I wanted to avoid the worst of the rush-hour traffic.

"I need to get going," I said.

"What about dinner?"

"We can do it at my place. I'll fix something when I get home."

Julianna smiled. "That would be great. After we eat, would you like a tour of the crime lab?"

"The crime lab? You mean, where you work?"

"Yes."

"Sounds fun," I said.

Julianna's job had intrigued me, and I thought it would be great to see it in person. I drove home, excited to learn more about her.

• • •

The forensic lab was a refurbished warehouse in the middle of an old Army depot. Amidst block-long warehouses, railroad tracks, and the shadow of a giant water tower was a small building with a sign that said Bureau of Forensic Sciences over the entrance. I had driven by the building many times, but had never paid much attention to it.

Julianna punched in a six-digit code to open the front door. The first room contained a large reception desk, two plastic chairs, and a potted plant.

"Do you get many visitors?" I said, half joking. I had expected the door to open to a fancy crime lab like I saw on the TV show CSI.

"Only law enforcement. This is where they drop off evidence for us to analyze," she said.

I followed Julianna around the back of the reception station, and she explained the process for admitting evidence to ensure chain of custody before being filed for analysis.

"Do you take in evidence and work in the lab?"

"I'll help if our intake person isn't in," Julianna said. "I was an intake tech when I started. It was the only job I could find after graduation. I almost didn't take it because it didn't require a college degree, but I knew it gave me the inside track for a future lab position. Six months after starting, a drug analyst opportunity opened up, and I got the job."

Julianna scanned her badge and punched in another code to another door. I followed her down a short hallway. This room was more like what I'd expected to see. Lab equipment covered long tables. Test tubes, flasks, and other scientific supplies filled cupboards. A shelf of elaborate bongs ringed the top of the room. Except for the bongs, everything was clean, white, and sterile.

"Is that your personal collection?" I said, motioning to the bongs.

Julianna laughed. "That's some of the more interesting evidence that we've collected over the years," she said. "You'd be surprised what gets turned in."

"What's one of the strangest things you've seen?"

Julianna thought for a moment. "One day, someone brought in a hollowed-out carrot that had been used to smoke marijuana."

"Really?"

"I don't think they were successful. They didn't hollow it out very well."

"Maybe they wanted a vitamin-infused high."

Julianna laughed, and we finished the tour of the lab. She showed me a gas chromatograph, a mass spectrometer, a comparison microscope, and other equipment. She explained how each machine worked, and how it analyzed drugs and other substances. Her explanations were factual and precise, but there was a passion in her words that only comes from someone who enjoys their job.

"What's with the pot plants?" I said, motioning to three plants on a windowsill.

"Oh, I'm growing them," she said. She said it in such a nonchalant way that I almost laughed.

"You grow marijuana?"

"It's part of my training. Growing them helps me identify samples when they're brought in."

"What else do you know how to do?" I found it intriguing that this straitlaced woman knew so much about drugs.

"I can cook meth."

"You're joking."

"All part of my training," she said.

"Guess if you ever run into financial trouble, you can start a drug business."

Julianna smiled. "I wouldn't be very good at that. I don't have a green thumb. You might not have noticed, but my marijuana plants aren't doing so well."

I laughed, then said, "On our first date, you mentioned something about examining body fluids. Are you still doing that?"

"I'm still cross-training in serology but it will take some time to get my certification."

"Do you find that more interesting than drugs?"

"It's more fulfilling," Julianna said. "With drugs, I just identify substances. I'm glad that I can help get those substances and some bad guys off the street, but helping solve rape cases or murders is more meaningful."

"Well, this lab is way more interesting than my job. If I gave you a tour it would just be cubicles and computers."

"There's more. Do you want to see the shooting range?"

"You have a shooting range?"

"The state's ballistic lab is located here. Want a look?"

"Yes," I said. Then, "What does it take to get a job here?"

"A hard science degree," she replied. "Interested in applying?"

"I don't know if my liberal arts brain could handle the math."

Julianna led me through another door to an unfinished part of the warehouse. Ahead was a room with a door. We stopped short of it, and Julianna pulled back a ten-by-ten-foot movable rack filled with guns. She pulled back a second rack and a third, revealing even more firearms. There were handguns, pistols, shotguns, and rifles of all sizes and calibers.

"Wow," I said.

"They're organized by cartridge, manufacturer, and type," Julianna explained.

"Does the state go out and buy every kind of gun?" I asked.

"Most of these weapons were seized from crime scenes."

"Why do you have so many of them?"

"Comparison purposes. Say you have a bullet casing but no gun, and want to know which weapon most likely fired it. Because each gun is unique, this can help identify the type of weapon. Sometimes guns come in with filed-off serial numbers. If our techs aren't familiar with the weapon, they can find the same make and model, and that gives them an idea of where to start."

Julianna pushed the racks back into place, then used a code to unlock the door to the shooting range. It looked like a typical indoor range. A bullet trap–where they could test-fire weapons and retrieve slugs–stood off to the side.

"Do you get to shoot the guns?" I asked.

"The other guys like to hone their shooting skills on their lunch breaks," Julianna said. "But I don't usually participate."

"Why not?"

"I understand and respect guns, but they're not my thing. Since working here, I've seen the consequences of people's poor decisions firsthand. Whether it's in the courtroom or in the evidence that comes through the lab, there are a lot of suffering people, broken families, and destroyed relationships because of these decisions."

My mind flashed back to hearing the gunshot and finding Krista's body. It took every ounce of my mental energy to push away the memory and accompanying feeling of horror.

The tour over, I followed Julianna through the lab and back outside. When we got to my car, she stopped and turned.

"On our first date, I said something about the damage a bullet can do to a human brain. You winced when I said it. At the time I thought it was because you were squeamish, but the real reason had to do with Krista's suicide, right?"

Another image of Krista's bloody, lifeless body entered my head. I nodded and pushed the image away.

"Why didn't you say anything?"

"I was trying to figure out the best way to break the widower news to you."

"I didn't mean to make you uncomfortable."

"You didn't know."

"I'm sorry if I brought back unpleasant memories."

"Don't worry about it," I said. "You wouldn't have said anything if you had known the details of her death."

"Still, I feel bad."

"Don't" I said. "I don't hold it against you." I decided to change the topic. "How are you doing with the me-being-sealed-to-Krista issue?"

"I'm still working through it."

"What does that mean?"

Julianna wrinkled her nose and looked at the ground. From what I knew of her body language, she had more to say but was uncertain or how to share it.

"Tell me what's on your mind," I said. "Your answer won't offend me." Julianna met my gaze then said, "I know it gives you comfort believing you'll be reunited with Krista and Hope in the next life but I find that thought agonizing. If Krista's there, where do I fit in?"

I opened my mouth, ready to tell Julianna that we sometimes didn't have a clear picture how things would work out in the next life and whatever our relationship looked like, she'd be happy. Not having a clear picture of the eternities but believing that everything would work out for the best was common Latter-day Saint advice for many issues. Friends and family had told me similar comments after Krista and Hope died. Their intent was to comfort me but their words had fallen flat, even though I knew what they were saying was true. Why would Julianna feel any different? Unsure what to say, I asked, "How do you think things will work out?"

Julianna bit her lower lip then said. "If I'm being honest, I have a hard time picturing the three of us together. When I think about the next life, I only see you and me."

I thought about Julianna's words and said, "You think that because Krista killed herself, I won't be married to her in the next life."

Julianna shrugged. "I don't know how things will work out, but I selfishly hope that it will just be you and me." She paused then asked, "Do you think you and Krista will be together?"

It was a good question, and one I had given a lot of thought to. Even though Krista and I were sealed in the temple, that didn't guarantee that our marriage or family relationship would last into the eternities—only that it has the potential to do so. Relationships continued in the next life only if husbands and wives live good lives here on earth. If we don't follow God's commandments, are unfaithful, or violate the promises we've made to each other and God, we won't be an eternal couple. While I knew Krista had lived a good life, her suicide had complicated matters.

I let out a slow breath. "Truthfully? I don't know."

Despite the rich and detailed doctrine of the Latter-day Saint faith, some questions remained unanswered. Latter-day Saint doctrine teaches that suicide is a sin, but that the Lord will judge those who take their own lives based on their unique circumstances. Most people interpret this to mean that those who have killed themselves because of—say, mental illness—will be judged less harshly than someone who does it intentionally. How Krista would fare for the circumstances of her death, I wasn't sure.

From the questioning way Julianna looked at me, she wanted me to explain my answer. A car drove past, loud music thumping from the speakers. I waited until the sound of the car and the music faded away before speaking.

"I don't know what she was thinking when she killed herself," I said. "I believe she deliberately waited until I got home to pull the trigger. Waiting for me to walk in the door is a calculated act—not one born of madness. However, I also believe there was an undiagnosed mental issue, like depression or some kind of pregnancy induced schizophrenia. How that all plays out in the next life, I don't know."

The bellow of a train horn sounded somewhere in the distance.

"I can't imagine what it's like to have that weighing on your mind," Julianna said.

I shrugged. "I used to think about it all the time. It consumed my thoughts. It still crosses my mind, but not as often. I can't waste my life worrying about something that's out of my control. Thankfully, I'm not the one who will judge her. All I can do is focus on moving forward and not making the same mistakes again."

We drove back to my house and spent the rest of the evening together. I don't remember how we spent the evening but I do remember thinking that I wanted to spend this life and the next with Julianna by my side. When it was time for her to leave, my self-control finally failed me. As she slipped on her shoes, I felt my heart go boom, boom, boom, and the words that were always top of mind finally slipped out.

"I love you," I said.

Everything went still. I wanted to claw my words out of the air and put them back in my mouth. Even though I meant them I wasn't sure this was the right time to say them.

Without missing a beat, Julianna said, "I love you too."

I hadn't expected that response, and I was too stunned to lean in and kiss her. But Julianna's crossed arms said she didn't want to be kissed. Instead, she took a step toward me and leaned her head against my chest and put her arms around me. I put my arms around her and held her tight. I could have stood there for hours, enjoying the warmth from her body and the faint smell of her flowery perfume.

At some point, we separated.

"Run tomorrow?" Julianna said.

"I'll be there at five," I replied.

I watched Julianna back out of my driveway and realized not everyone got a second chance at love. I had missed opportunities to save my relationship with Krista and vowed not to repeat those same mistakes with Julianna.

CHAPTER TWENTY-ONE

Julianna

I was thrilled when Abel uttered the words "I love you." Although his actions—running with me in the mornings and taking down photos of Krista—had shown that he loved me, I cherished the verbal confirmation. I could see us getting married, raising a family, and growing old together. But I still had so many unanswered questions about Krista—and Abel still wore his wedding band.

Asking Abel to refer to Krista as something other than his wife had been difficult. But discussing a symbol of Abel's love and marriage to Krista reached a completely different level. I needed guidance. Did most widowers continue wearing their wedding band? Should I ask Abel to remove it or learn to live with it? What was the best way to address the topic without coming across as jealous or petty? I wanted to ask my dad, but I felt like this topic was beyond his realm of expertise. Google searches were of no help either. The only person who would have answers was God, so I prayed about what to say to Abel about his wedding ring every night. While waiting for an answer I hoped Abel might take off his wedding band the way he had taken down the photos of Krista: without me saying anything. But each time I found an excuse to touch or brush my hand against his chest, the bump remained.

Then one Sunday morning I drove to Salt Lake for a cousin's missionary homecoming. Homecomings are a chance for newly returning missionaries to speak in church about their experiences from their mission. My cousin had spent the last two years in Brazil and I was looking forward to seeing him again and hearing his stories.

I wanted to invite Abel, but I didn't. My parents, sisters, and most of my extended family would be there and I didn't want to make introductions until I had some answers. On the drive I pictured Abel in the passenger seat asking about my family, sharing stories from his mission in Bulgaria, and discussing our running schedule for the week. Despite trying to come to grips with his marriage to Krista, the fact we had yet to kiss, and no clear indication that Abel was ready to make me number one in his heart, I loved him.

I had finally accepted that Abel would never stop loving Krista, but I couldn't marry him if he continued wearing the ring. I couldn't spend my life competing with a ghost. I also didn't want him to feel forced into something he wasn't ready for—whether that was removing the ring or moving forward with me.

I thought of all the experiences Abel had with Krista. Marriage. Intimacy. A child. Firsts for me, seconds for him. If we married and had children of our own, would he always compare his new life to his old one? What if Krista was a better wife? A better lover? Would that tear our marriage apart? The questions tore at my soul until I arrived at the church. At least for the next hour, I could focus on my cousin.

My reprieve didn't last long. As I entered the chapel my mom waved me over to a seat she had saved. The moment I sat down, she peppered me with questions.

"You didn't bring Abel?" Her tone landed somewhere between surprise and disappointment.

"You'll meet him soon," I replied even though I didn't know when or if that would happen. If this had been a normal relationship—one without the widower complications—he would have met my family soon after we became exclusive.

"Are things still moving forward?"

"Yes," I said even though I wanted to tell her, "Recently I found out he still wears his wedding band on a chain around his neck and I can't decide how I should approach it or give him time to take it off."

I didn't share those details because I needed more than a sympathetic ear. I needed advice from someone who had been in my shoes, someone who could truly relate to how I was feeling.

The questioning continued.

"Is he still running with you?"

"Every morning."

"Is he getting faster?"

"He's keeping up with me."

"It takes a special guy to want to run with you every day."

"I know."

"When are you going to bring him by to meet the family?"

The service started before I could answer, effectively ending our conversation. I tried to focus on the prayers, hymns, and sacrament but my mind kept drifting back to Abel, his wedding band, Krista's pictures on the wall, feeling like second place, and what our relationship would look like in the eternities. When my cousin spoke, I pushed aside my worries and concerns and focused on his message.

He told some humorous stories and spiritual experiences about his two years in Brazil. He was a great storyteller which helped keep thoughts of Abel at bay. As he wrapped up his talk, he mentioned the importance of families and told a story about being in the celestial room—the highest and holiest place in Latter-day Saint temples—with his parents, sisters, and brothers and the joy and peace he felt with them all together in this room.

As my cousin described this experience, his voice faded away. My family and the chapel blurred into the background as a warm feeling filled my body. As the feeling grew stronger, thoughts entered my mind as if someone was speaking the words directly to me. The words were clear and direct.

Marrying Abel is a choice. If you choose to marry him, one day you, Abel, and your children will all be in the celestial room of the temple together. With Abel you can have an eternal family and experience all the joy, happiness, and blessings that accompany this. It is your choice to have an eternal relationship with him.

A powerful, peaceful feeling accompanied these thoughts, and all my concerns and worries about Abel vanished. This was the answer to my prayers, only it wasn't the answer I had expected. I wanted a clear-cut "yes" or "no" about whether I should marry Abel. I wanted to know exactly what the next life would look like with Krista, or if she'd be part of it. Instead, I received a choice—a relationship with Abel was my decision.

If I proceeded, it would be without knowing how things would work out in the eternities.

I sat pondering these thoughts. The next thing I knew, the service was over. The congregation and my family milled around the chapel or lined up to visit with my cousin. And just as suddenly, I was back in my car, driving to Ogden, trying to process the revelation I'd had in the chapel.

As I drove, my mind returned to a prompting I had received my sophomore year at the University of Puget Sound. At the beginning of the winter semester, I felt I needed to return home and finish my chemistry degree at the University of Utah. This out-of-the-blue impression came one day as I finished up math homework at the university's library. The prompting was so strong I stopped working on my equations.

Why did I need to go back to Utah? At UPS, I had great professors, good friends, and I liked my studies. Plus, I enjoyed the wet and temperate climate of the Pacific Northwest more than dry, dusty Utah. Switching schools made no logical sense. Besides, the life I envisioned after graduating included applying to medical school and living in the Seattle area. Returning home would complicate those plans.

For several days I mused about what to do. My parents and church leaders taught me to follow spiritual promptings no matter how odd they seemed. I had done my best to heed them but I struggled with this one. I discussed returning home with my parents and prayed about my next steps. Eventually I decided to follow the impression and return home when the school year ended. The decision stunned my college advisor and professors. They offered me more scholarships, financial aid, and other incentives to stay, dramatically lowering the cost of tuition and other expenses for my last two years of school. I second-guessed my decision to leave, but ultimately, I moved back to Utah.

The hardest part was not knowing why I should return. My mind craved logic and certainty. That was one reason why I enjoyed chemistry. Chemical reactions, formulas, and equations didn't change and can be reproduced in a lab. Hydrogen always has one electron. Helium always has two. A water molecule is comprised of two hydrogen atoms and one oxygen atom. If you expose iron to oxygen and water, you get rust.

Faith doesn't work that way. While it's possible to get answers to questions through prayer, study, and meditation, often spiritual promptings come without any real knowing. Moving back home would have been easier if I'd known it would lead to a better job after graduation, improve my chances of going to medical school, or result in meeting my future husband. Despite many prayers, I never received a reason for the move.

Once I returned home, it didn't take long to second-guess my decision. The chemistry program at the University of Utah was subpar. The program and classes were bigger and less personal. Most professors cared more about their academic careers than their students. And my dating life changed little. Most days I felt that my academic and social life had suffered. Some days, I wished I'd stayed at Puget Sound. Despite these setbacks, I continued my schooling and hoped that one day the reason for the prompting would appear, but when I graduated two years later, I still didn't have an answer.

•••

Lost in my thoughts, the drive went by quickly and I exited the freeway. I could continue to my apartment or drive to Abel's house. Half of me needed time and space to think about my next steps but the other half wanted to see Abel again.

At the last second, I picked Abel. I parked in his driveway, and stared out the windshield at nothing, thinking about Abel, his wedding band, Krista, and the next life. Still in a fog, I got out of the car.

Abel opened the door before I knocked.

"How was the homecoming?" he asked, holding the door open for me.

"Great," I replied, stepping inside. "It was nice to see my cousin again. How was church?"

"I like it better when you're with me," Abel said. "Have you had lunch? We could make some sandwiches if you're hungry."

I should have been hungry but thoughts of a future with Abel overwhelmed my need to eat. I agreed to lunch anyway and helped Abel prepare the meal. As we stood next to each other cutting cheese and tomatoes, I realized how natural it felt to do a simple thing like making lunch together. I liked that feeling.

As we ate, Abel talked about something he'd learned at church. While he spoke, I thought about our future and for the second time that day I envisioned a long, happy life together. But when my thoughts focused on the eternities, things got blurry. Could I move forward without all the answers?

We finished lunch and carried our dishes to the sink. As I rinsed off my plate, Abel set his dishes on the counter, stood directly behind me, and placed his hands on my hips. I closed my eyes and leaned against him, enjoying the feeling of our bodies pressed together. I knew if I turned around, Abel would kiss me. I rested the back of my head against his chest unsure if I was ready to take that step.

You don't have to do this, I reminded myself. *You can marry someone else. Someone who doesn't have a wife in the next life.*

My mind returned to the answer I'd received earlier and the peaceful feeling that still engulfed my soul. If I was to move forward with Abel, now was the time to commit.

Abel squeezed my hips, inviting me to turn around. I took a deep breath and let him turn me so we faced each other.

He leaned down to kiss me.

I met him halfway.

Our lips touched, soft and delicate, like flower petals. I closed my eyes and my heart beat faster as I inhaled Abel's scent. I felt the warmth of his body against mine, as we enjoyed a long, tender kiss.

CHAPTER TWENTY-TWO

Abel

It was thrilling and terrifying to be in a committed relationship again. I wanted everyone to know that Julianna and I were exclusive, but I was unsure how family and friends would react. Most of them were still grieving Krista's death, and emotions were raw. I didn't want to lose friendships over my decision, but I couldn't let others' sorrow stop me from starting a new chapter. The relationship with Julianna would continue with or without their support.

I told my parents first because they practically lived next door. Julianna spent enough time at my place that I was sure they had seen her car in my driveway, though I doubted they knew the extent of our dating. I would have preferred to share the good news with Julianna at my side, but the shock and horror on my mom's face when she learned about my dating activities was fresh on my mind. I didn't want Julianna witnessing a less-than-positive reaction. I wanted to include Julianna in future activities with my family, but I wouldn't expose her to situations where she would feel like an intruder or interloper. I remembered their celebratory reaction when I told them Krista and I were exclusive and hoped that this news would bring the same joy and approval.

I found my parents in the backyard sitting around the firepit. A trickle of blue-gray smoke rose lazily into the still summer air. My mom's face brightened when she noticed me.

"Abel, it's been a while since we've seen you. Have a seat and tell us what you've been up to."

Instead of taking a seat, I put my hands on the back of a plastic lawn chair. Sitting was the last thing I wanted to do.

"Giving you an update on my life is why I'm here," I said, trying to keep my voice upbeat. Maybe a positive tone would help ease the news.

"Oh?" my mom said.

"You may have noticed Julianna Taylor's car at my house a lot. Just wanted you to know that the two of us are dating exclusively."

My dad stroked his beard with his hand, but said little. I had expected this reaction. In order to form an opinion about Julianna, he'd have to meet her. My mom nodded stoically, which in my mind was a win. The conversation was short and to the point, and I was relieved when it was over. To my surprise, my dad walked me home. On the way back, he showered me with questions. What did Julianna do for a living? Where did I see the relationship going? When was I going to introduce her to the family? There was an excitement to his voice, and I took his questions as a sign that he was supportive of me moving forward. I answered my dad's questions and told him I'd introduce Julianna to the family soon.

As difficult as that conversation was, it wasn't anything compared to telling Krista's grandmother and brother. Though I had stayed in regular contact with them since Krista's death, I had said nothing to them about dating or Julianna. If they were going to learn that I was in an exclusive relationship, I wanted it to come from me—not from someone else.

I went over to their house a few days later when Scott had a day off from work. Pulling into their driveway, I realized I hadn't been there since Julianna and I started running together. For months after Krista's death, I had stopped by once a week or so to check in on them and catch up, but those visits had gone by the wayside as spending time with Julianna had become my main priority.

Scott answered the door wearing a T-shirt and shorts. In his early twenties, he had the same blonde hair and blue eyes as his sister, and seeing him triggered memories of playing video games and target shooting together. He was Krista's only sibling, and I had liked him as a brother-in-law. I wondered how the news about Julianna would affect our relationship.

"Hey, Abel," he said, opening the door. "You don't have to knock. This is your house too."

After Krista and I tied the knot, there was an unspoken rule that I didn't have to knock at Loretta's door. Her house was open to me like it was to Krista and her brother. It was a rule I followed during our marriage, but today with the news I was about to share, it felt wrong.

"I didn't call before coming over," I said. "Didn't want to surprise everyone."

Scott held the door open, and I stepped inside. Loretta's home was an orange brick nine-hundred-square-foot home that was built in the 1950s. Krista and Scott had spent most of their youth growing up in this home, as their mentally ill parents were unable to adequately care for them full time. As I passed through the kitchen, memories of playing cards at the table and eating Sunday dinner together flashed through my mind. As I passed into the living room, I noticed the door to Krista's former bedroom was open. Scott had taken it over as his own after Krista moved out, but I could see beyond his computer, stereo, and unmade bed to remember Krista's pink bedspread, the stack of books on her nightstand, and a white jewelry box on her chest of drawers like it was yesterday.

Loretta was sitting in an easy chair in the living room. She turned off the TV, and a smile broke across her face when I entered. She stood and gave me a hug.

"I'm glad you stopped by," she said, motioning to the couch. "It's been several weeks since we talked. How are you doing?"

I took a seat on the couch, and the three of us spent a few minutes catching up. We talked about my job, the new ward Loretta attended, and Scott's college math class. It felt like a normal conversation—the kind we had before Krista died—and one I would have enjoyed more if it wasn't for the heavy feeling in my stomach.

Finally, our conversation reached a pause, and I said, "There's something I need to let both of you know."

The room grew quiet, and I could tell by the perplexed looks on their faces that they were unsure where the conversation was going. I had rehearsed my words many times, but the well-practiced lines vanished from my memory. Instead, I said, "For the last few months, I've been dating. Recently I've become serious with someone, and if things continue, we're probably going to get married."

Silence filled the room, but I didn't take that as a bad sign. I had just told Krista's brother and grandmother that I was dating again and opening my heart to another woman in the same sentence. It was a lot to digest. I scoured their faces to see how they were taking the news. Scott cocked his head to one side and rubbed his forehead. Loretta's expression was harder to read, but her knuckles turned white from gripping the armrests of her chair.

The silence continued until Scott said, "Is she someone I know?"

I shook my head. "I don't think so. Her name is Julianna. She moved into your old ward back in January. We've been dating since the ward split."

More silence.

"And you're going to marry her," Scott said.

"The relationship is heading in that direction. I wanted you to hear it from me instead of the rumor mill," I said. "I also want you both to know that I still love Krista more than words can express. She was an amazing woman, and her sweet influence will always be a part of me."

Loretta wiped a tear from the corner of her eye with the back of her hand. "Thank you for telling us. I'm glad you're moving forward with your life. You were a good husband to Krista, and I know you'll be one for Julianna."

She meant it as a compliment, but her words felt like a punch in the gut. If I had been a good husband, Krista would still be alive. I pushed past the guilt and focused my attention back on Loretta and Scott.

Scott stared at the floor and said nothing.

"Julianna studied chemistry. She's good at math. If you need help with your class, she could probably give you some tips."

"Yeah, maybe," Scott said.

Loretta asked a few questions about Julianna, and I left a few minutes later. As I got in my car, instead of feeling relieved, I felt sad. No matter how things turned out with Julianna, my relationship with Loretta and Scott would never be the same. I could never again walk into Loretta's house without knocking first.

Backing out of the driveway, I glanced at the living room window and wondered what was going through their minds. They had lost a sister and a granddaughter. Did the news about Julianna make them feel like they were losing me, too? I didn't know what role either of them would play in my life going forward, but found it ironic that what had changed the relationship wasn't Krista's death, but me falling in love with someone else. The feeling of loss weighed heavily on my shoulders weeks after the conversation, and I wondered if the feeling would ever fully go away.

•••

Julianna and I were unsure how to let everyone at church know we were a couple. Did we arrive and sit together and let the rumor mill start? Should we walk in holding hands and announce it to people we saw? Neither of us had an answer. The one thing we were both sure of was that the news would spread through the congregation like wildfire.

My only concern was the reactions from members of the congregation who were close to Krista. While neither Julianna nor I cared what other people thought, I wanted church to be a place where we felt comfortable attending. Even though we were moving forward together publicly, I knew Julianna still had questions about the afterlife and was still trying to make sure I was ready to start a new chapter of my life with her. I worried that if attending the ward became a source of discomfort, our relationship would crumble.

The Saturday before we attended church together as a couple, I took Julianna to a nearby Greek restaurant for dinner. The server brought our food, and we ate in silence as we were both hungry from the fifty miles we had run that week. At some point, I felt like someone was watching us. I looked around and spotted Brother and Sister Davis, a middle-aged couple who attended our church, two tables over. Brother Davis was looking right at us, a big smile on his face. Our eyes met, and he gave me a knowing nod. He said something to his wife, and she glanced in our direction. She did a double take, a surprised look on her face.

"So, how do you think people at church are going to react tomorrow when they learn the two of us are dating?" I asked, turning my attention back to Julianna.

She swallowed her food and wiped her mouth with a napkin. "I hope they don't have a problem with it," she said. "Why?"

With my head, I motioned toward the Davises.

It took her a moment to recognize them, but her eyes went wide and she gave them a smile and wave.

"I think word is going to spread pretty fast," I said.

Julianna reached across the table and took my hand in hers. "Not only have they seen us having dinner together, but now they've seen us holding hands. What a scandal! We're going to be the talk of the ward tomorrow."

A laugh started in my belly and worked its way out my mouth. At that moment, I realized that no matter how people reacted, it wouldn't affect Julianna or our relationship.

I squeezed her hand and said, "I guess that means we're sitting by each other tomorrow at church."

"Sitting together and holding hands," she said.

We burst into laughter and finished our meal. We gave Brother and Sister Davis a wave and held our hands high for them to see on our way out the door.

After dinner, we headed to the Weber County Fair. My dad had given me two extra tickets, and it seemed like a nice way to end the week. Soon after arriving, we ran into a young married couple from our ward. After exchanging small talk, the wife noticed we were holding hands.

"Are you two dating?" she asked.

"Yes," Julianna and I said at the same time.

We looked at each other and laughed.

"How wonderful!" she exclaimed. "I didn't know you guys were a couple. How long have you two been together?"

We gave them the relationship rundown before going our separate ways. The encounter left me with a smile on my face. There was something about being open about our relationship that made me love Julianna more.

A few minutes later, we ran into more people from church. Like the previous encounter, they were surprised to see us together, but they expressed nothing but happiness and excitement at the news. Random encounters with other ward members went on all evening and by the time we left, it seemed like we had bumped into half the congregation. It made me confident that when we showed up at church together the next morning, it would be a positive experience.

And it was.

We arrived ten minutes early and walked into the chapel holding hands. I could feel the stares of those who were already in the pews as we walked down the aisle, but kept my attention focused on Julianna. We sat in her usual pew near the front.

The most surprised reaction came from the bishop—the congregation's lay leader—and his two counselors who were sitting on the stand, waiting for the service to begin. One counselor tapped the bishop on the arm as we took our seats. The bishop did a double take. We smiled at them as we took our seats and watched as they smiled back and started talking amongst themselves.

After the service, several members of the congregation approached us to ask if we were dating, then expressed their happiness that we were. I don't think either of us could have envisioned a more positive reaction. As we drove back to my place after church, I realized that outside forces would not stop us from being together. It was up to us to overcome our concerns and keep things moving forward.

CHAPTER TWENTY-THREE

Julianna

Abel met my parents and sisters the following weekend. Everyone liked him, and he took some good-natured teasing from my younger sisters in stride. From that day on, he accompanied me on Saturday morning runs that stretched across the Salt Lake Valley, and our lives became fully integrated with each other. The only time we were apart was during work and bedtime.

My love for Abel deepened, and I looked forward to spending the rest of our lives together and having a family. But there was still one issue that needed to be resolved: his wedding band. I wondered if Abel was even aware of it. Occasionally, I saw him trace the ring under his shirt with a finger, but it appeared to be a subconscious act. Because I had said nothing about it, he probably didn't know it bothered me. We needed to talk about it or nothing would change.

Discussing these unique issues was something we were still learning to navigate. Recently, after our morning run, we were drinking cold glasses of water and making plans for the evening.

"What if we had dinner at my place tonight?" I suggested.

"That sounds great, Krista," Abel replied. His eyes widened, and he immediately corrected himself. "I mean, Julie." He set his glass on the counter and looked at his watch. "I've got to go or I'll be late for work."

Abel was out the door before I could fully process what he had said. Had he called me Krista? My mind went into overdrive. Why had he called me Krista? Was it a slip of the tongue, or did it mean he didn't love me? Why had he rushed out the door? Embarrassment? Something else? As I showered and dressed for work, these questions pinged around my mind. They were going to drive me crazy unless I got some answers. I called my dad and explained what happened.

"Why did he call me Krista?" I asked.

"I don't know," my dad said, "but if you want this relationship to work out, you need to talk about this and other issues as they come up. These problems don't solve themselves."

I knew my dad was right, but what was the best way to bring up the topic? The possible fallout worried me more than the actual conversation. What if Abel admitted he still loved Krista more than me, or had second thoughts about our relationship? I reminded myself that I was probably overthinking things, but when Abel didn't make his usual call or send an email during work hours to check in on me, I panicked.

Maybe he's busy at work or too embarrassed about what happened, I told myself. My thoughts did little to calm my worries.

Abel came over while I was in the middle of making spaghetti and meatballs. He walked in with a smile on his face. "Dinner smells great," he said.

Though his relaxed demeanor helped ease my worries, my heart still hammered in my chest. "We need to talk," I said, motioning to the couch. "Have a seat."

Abel's smile faded, and he took a seat on one end of the couch. "What's up?"

I sat on the middle cushion so we were still close. I placed my hands on my knees and asked, "Why did you call me Krista this morning?"

"Oh, you heard that?" Abel said.

I nodded.

"Slip of the tongue."

"Were you thinking about her?"

"Not really."

"Why did you call me her name?"

Abel took a moment to answer. On the stove, I heard water boiling in the pot, but ignored it. This conversation was too important.

"I don't know how to explain it."

"Try," I said.

Abel ran his hands through his hair. "I'm very comfortable with you," he said. "I mean, really comfortable. Most days, it feels like our lives are one."

This seemed positive. I waited for him to continue.

"I had the same ease and comfort with Krista," he continued. "This morning, the comfort felt like it did when I was with her.

I wasn't thinking of her—just that I felt happy and content in a similar way."

I thought over what Abel had said, understanding this to be a good thing. At least, I hoped it was. I agreed that our lives were merging in a happy, cozy way, though I had nothing to compare it to.

"I'm sorry I called you Krista," Abel said. "I'll try to do better going forward."

I accepted his apology, and he helped fix dinner. We moved on to other things, and by the end of the evening, things seemed back to normal.

Despite our improvement in talking about small issues, his wedding band was bigger. What if Abel refused to remove the ring? Was I strong enough to hold my ground and walk away from the relationship, or would I fold and settle? Besides, this wasn't a conversation about a slip of the tongue, but something that symbolized Abel's love and commitment to Krista. It was deeply personal.

Weeks passed, and the ring remained. Finally, I reached a breaking point. We were driving back to Ogden one Saturday after a run that took us from the Bingham Copper Mine to my parents' home in Taylorsville. I glanced over at Abel and noticed him tracing the outline of the ring with his index finger of his right hand. His left hand rested on the wheel. Whether the action was intentional or subconscious, I didn't know. However, I couldn't keep quiet any longer. I had to say something.

"Do you think you're ready to open your heart?" I said.

"I believe so," Abel said.

"I don't think you're ready to move forward," I replied. The words rushed out of my mouth like wind from a canyon.

Abel's head snapped toward me. "What?"

It was too late to take it back. I was about to tell him how much the ring bothered me, but then I had a strong impression that I shouldn't mention it. I took a deep breath and said, "I don't think you're completely ready to open your heart."

Abel sat up straight in his seat and gripped the steering wheel with both hands. "What are you talking about?"

I desperately wanted to tell Abel about the ring, but something told me I should keep it vague. That went against everything I knew about open and honest communication. If there was an issue to discuss, you needed to speak up and tell that person in a kind but firm way. But I trusted my feeling and kept it nebulous.

"There's still some work you need to do," I said.

"I ran sixteen miles with you this morning," Abel said. "I wouldn't do that for just anyone."

"This isn't about the run," I said. "It's something else."

"Okay—what is it, then?"

For the second time I felt I shouldn't address it directly. I tried to think of a subtle hint, but my mind was blank. Instead, I replied, "You're not quite ready."

"If there's something I need to do, tell me what it is," Abel said. There was a hint of frustration in his voice.

Abel was right. I should tell him how much the symbol of his love for Krista bothered me. I took a moment to compose my thoughts, then said, "Trust me on this. There's still more you need to do."

Abel spent the next five miles trying to convince me to open up, but I didn't give in. Finally, he settled back in his seat and bit his lower lip. We drove the rest of the way to Ogden in silence, and I second-guessed my decision not to mention the ring. Abel dropped me off and went back to his place for the night.

Back at my apartment, I wondered if he would figure out what he still needed to work through. All I could do was hope that following those promptings would lead to something good. I hoped that Abel would call and want to talk it out more, but the phone remained silent.

In the end, I sat alone in my apartment, reading a book. It was the first time in a month I'd spent the evening by myself. Before Abel came into my life, I looked forward to Saturday nights, when I could read, make myself a shake—my reward for a week of hard work and marathon training. This should have been one of those nights, but I found it impossible to relax or lose myself in the latest Patricia Cornwell novel. I missed Abel and wished he was sitting next to me. Several times I thought about calling and inviting him over for a treat or a movie, but my gut told me to give him space. He had worked through other issues and I felt confident he could find the strength to remove his wedding band.

But what if he couldn't take it off? I reminded myself that a relationship with Abel was my choice. I didn't have to continue down this path if he couldn't make me number one. Even though I wanted to marry him, I couldn't go through with it if I felt like second best. Removing the wedding band had to be something Abel did on his own—not because I asked him. It was the only way I could see our relationship continuing.

• • •

The next morning, Abel picked me up for church. He seemed more distant than usual, but maybe I was reading too much into the situation. I kept looking at Abel's chest to see if he had taken off the ring, but the white shirt and tie made it impossible to tell. Occasionally, I glanced over to see if he was subconsciously fiddling with it, but I never saw his hand on his chest. I decided to address the issue later in the day.

After church, Abel dropped me off. I changed into jeans and a blouse, then drove over to his house for lunch. Abel had changed into a T-shirt with a high neck, and I couldn't tell if he was wearing the chain. We ate, then went for a walk hand in hand around the neighborhood. We told jokes, discussed upcoming morning runs, and planned some evening activities. I kept looking at his neck and torso, but couldn't tell if the ring was there. After the walk, we ended up on the couch talking, flirting, and occasionally kissing. I was happy that our relationship was still moving forward.

At some point, there was a lull in the conversation, and Abel's expression became serious. He looked me directly in the eyes and said, "I thought a lot about our conversation yesterday. You know, the one about me not being ready to open my heart."

My body stiffened, and the atmosphere in the room changed from fun and flirty to serious and sober.

"Oh?" I said, trying to sound as nonchalant as possible.

"I was upset that you wouldn't tell me what was bothering you," Abel said.

I cringed, not having realized that the conversation had made him unhappy. I studied his face, but he didn't appear angry.

Abel continued, "I'm doing everything in my ability to move forward, and it's hard to hear that you see things differently."

I looked at Abel's chest for a sign of the telltale bump. The T-shirt was scrunched up, making it impossible to tell what was under it. I checked his neck for a sign of the chain, but the crewneck collar rode high, obscuring my view.

Abel continued. "After you dropped me off, I was about to get in the shower when I noticed my wedding ring, and I wondered if that might be what you were talking about."

Without thinking, my hand shot toward his chest. Abel caught my hand in his and held it a few inches above his shirt.

"I removed the ring," Abel said.

Gently, he placed my hand on his heart. Slowly I searched every inch of chest, feeling for the bump of his wedding band.

It was gone.

Tears started in the corners of my eyes, and I threw my arms around Abel.

"Thank you. Thank you," I said. "You don't know how much this means to me."

"Why didn't you just tell me to take it off?" Abel said. "I would have done it."

"I felt it was something you needed to figure out on your own."

"I don't want anything from my past to come between us," Abel said. "I want to start a new life, and I want it to be with you."

I felt Abel's chest again, then said, "What did you do with the ring?"

"I put it in Krista's jewelry box next to her wedding ring."

We had a long kiss, then I placed my head on Abel's chest.

I felt the rise and fall, slow and steady, with each breath and listened to the rhythmic thump thump thump of his heart. With his wedding band gone, I could feel him and just him. It was wonderful not having anything between us.

CHAPTER TWENTY-FOUR

Abel

One evening in late September we sat on the couch, tired from long hours at work and an eight-mile run that morning. Julianna rested her head on my shoulder, and her right arm crossed my torso like a seatbelt. The bright orange and yellow leaves from the trees across the street filled the window. The leaves danced from side to side in the breeze. Occasionally one or two would fall from their branch and flutter out of view.

Instead of enjoying the fall colors, my thoughts were on spending the rest of my life with Julianna. We had never discussed marriage, but in my mind it was a matter of when, not if. We ate, ran errands, bought groceries, did laundry, along with all the other minute, day-to-day tasks together. We spent so much time with each other that in many ways it felt like we were already married and I hoped to make it official as soon as possible.

I wanted to talk with Julianna about what our married life would look like but I lacked the courage to start the conversation. Julianna mentioned she received an answer to her prayers, but she was still working through some widower and afterlife concerns. I wanted to be certain I was emotionally and mentally ready to marry Julianna. My love and anger for Krista were still strong. Though I had processed some of my grief and worked hard to forgive her, I still had work to do. But sitting there, watching the leaves twist and bounce in the wind, felt like a good time to ask some questions.

"What temple do you want to get married in?" I asked, trying to drop the question casually. It was customary to let the woman pick the temple and it seemed like every woman had a favorite.

"Bountiful," Julianna said without any hesitation.

"Why that one?"

"I remember being excited when it was announced then driving to the construction site with my family several times. It was the first temple I walked through when it was open to the public so it has a special place in my heart."

"It's a beautiful temple," I said.

I waited a moment before asking the next question.

"Where do you want to live after we're married?" The question assumed that we were going to get married at some point in the future and I was curious how she would respond.

Julianna raised her head from my shoulder. "I don't know," she said. "Did you have somewhere in mind?"

A surge of excitement filled my body. She hadn't pushed back about the thought of us spending our lives together.

"I figure the options are my house, your apartment, or somewhere new," I said.

"I like the idea of somewhere new."

This took me by surprise. Though I didn't care where we lived, I assumed she'd pick either my place or hers.

"Why somewhere new?"

Julianna paused before speaking. During the previous months, I'd come to realize she sometimes needed to figure out how to articulate her response as diplomatically as possible. This usually happened when discussing Krista or relationship issues.

"I think it's best to start our marriage in a neutral location," she finally said.

"What do you mean by neutral?"

"One that's not so heavily associated with memories of the past. A place where both of us can start fresh."

"Does this house feel like Krista's home?"

Julianna shook her head. "No, but you mentioned it was her dream to buy this home and fix it up. Even though she never lived here, in some ways it feels like her place."

"Makes sense, though I should point out that the mortgage is dirt cheap."

"I'll take that into consideration after you propose," she said smiling.

Her words thrilled me. The fact that she saw a proposal in the future made me believe she was working through her concerns faster than I thought.

Julianna sat up straighter, as if the conversation had energized her. "Since we're talking marriage, how many kids do you want?" she asked.

My mind pinged back to the time when Krista and I had a similar conversation. I wanted a big family but Krista only wanted one or two children. Family size was something we had never agreed on and I had hoped that after we had our first child Krista would be open to having more. Given a second chance, I wanted to marry someone who also wanted lots of kids. What if Julianna also wanted a small family? Could I settle a second time?

"Lots," I said. "You?"

"A bunch," Julianna replied.

"Give me a number," I said,

"As many as we can have. Is that a problem?"

"Not at all," I replied. "I think it's wonderful. It's just that most people don't want large families."

"We'll figure out the right number as we go," Julianna said.

I was relieved she didn't want to get bogged down in a numbers discussion. What was important was we both wanted a big family.

Since the conversation was flowing, I asked more questions.

"What about your job? What would you like to do once we become parents?"

This was another issue that Krista and I had butted heads over and never resolved.

"If we have a lot of kids, I don't see how I could work. I'd prefer to stay home while they're young and figure something out once they're all in school or out of the house."

Once again Julianna and I were in complete alignment.

We kept talking. We discussed finances, sex, and parenting strategies. We saw eye-to-eye on practically everything. The next thing I knew it was dark outside and Julianna stood to grab her car keys off the kitchen table. We had stayed up later than normal and had a six-mile run in the morning. I kissed her goodnight.

"I love you," I said.

"I love you more," Julianna said, a playful lilt in her voice.

"I love you most times eternity."

Julianna paused and said, "I love you most times eternity too."

We kissed again.

As I readied for bed, I replayed our conversation in my mind. The only marriage-related topic we didn't discuss was the proposal (that would fall on me) and when we would join our lives together. Our conversations hadn't treated marriage as something that *might* happen but rather something that *would* happen. So that night when I went to bed, I thought about when to pop the question.

•••

After our fourteen-mile Saturday run, Julianna agreed to look at rings. She liked tension diamonds and white gold look but everything that fit that description were too grandiose or flashy. Julianna wanted something simple. We visited a store where she actually found a few rings she liked but her face didn't light up when she tried them on and I could tell she wasn't in love with them. I made some mental notes of the ones she preferred and made plans to come back and look at them again on Monday. On the drive home, I thought of different ways to pop the question and when to do it. The only big event on our calendar was the St. George Marathon that Julianna was running in the beginning of October and I weighed the pros and cons of proposing the days before or the days after the race.

As if reading my mind Julianna said, "When you ask me to marry you, I have one request."

Her words jolted me from my proposal fantasies.

"What's that?" I said. Previously Julianna had mentioned that she didn't like public proposals. That meant places like restaurants or sporting events were off limits. She wanted something private and intimate which was fine with me. I thought Julianna was going to remind me of that. Instead, she said something unexpected.

"I'd prefer that you wait until it has been a year to propose."

Wait a year? I didn't understand. Was she talking about waiting until the New Year? A year from our first date? Something else?

"What do you mean?" I didn't want to wait long. I'd marry her tomorrow, if it was possible.

Julianna shook her head. "I want you to wait until it has been at least a year since Krista died."

"Oh," I said.

Julianna had a worried look on her face as if her request might offend me. And it had. A little.

Though I had considered crossing that milestone before asking, losing Krista had taught me how precious life and relationships were. I wanted to get married sooner rather than later. At the same time, I knew I had to respect Julianna's needs. I wanted the proposal to be something she would remember fondly. I didn't want it tainted by negative thoughts or feelings. If Julianna wanted me to wait until after the anniversary of Krista's death, I'd wait. Besides, she was only asking me to wait another seven weeks—not seven years.

In Latter-day Saint culture, most people date for about a year before marriage. This has to do with two things: the faith's focus on sexual abstinence before marriage and intentional dating. Most of my friends who had married in the temple had tied the knot within twelve months of their first date.

I reached over and took Julianna's hand. "If it's important to wait until then, I'll wait," I said.

Julianna squeezed my hand. "Thanks. I can't wait to spend the rest of our lives and eternity together."

"Is it really going to happen?" I said the words playfully to hide my worries that ultimately marrying a widower was something she couldn't do.

"So long as we keep moving forward," she said.

I let her words roll around my head for a minute.

"Forward together," I said.

"Together," she replied.

"I love you most times eternity."

"I love you most times eternity, too."

I squeezed her hand back and wondered what, if any, difference waiting would make.

• • •

Monday, I took a long lunch and returned to the jewelry store. The salesperson remembered me and together we looked at the rings Julianna seemed to prefer. Each ring had most of the qualities she wanted but there was also something missing. A gorgeous tension diamond was yellow gold. A white gold one was too ornate. The simpler looking rings didn't have anything close to a tension look. If we were going to spend the rest of our lives together, I wanted her to have something she loved whenever she looked at it.

"I don't think any of these will work," I told the salesperson.

"We did get a shipment of rings in this morning," she said. "If you want, we can see if there's something that will work in the back."

"Sure," I said. "What can it hurt?" I wasn't optimistic she'd find anything but I didn't see the harm in looking at other rings.

She returned a few minutes later with two rings. One with a white gold band and round diamond embedded in the middle—caught my eye. Though it wasn't a tension diamond, it looked like one. The best part was that the ring itself had a simple, sleek look. My gut told me Julianna would love the ring and I bought it on the spot.

That night I lay on my bed, watched the diamond sparkle in the light, and imagined different ways of proposing. At some point my attention drifted to Krista's graduation photo and my mind went back to what life had been like a year earlier. It was around this time when Krista's emotional health had spiraled downward at a fast clip and the woman who was looking forward to being a mother became increasingly dark and despondent. The woman who was a dependable employee quit her job without notifying her employer or me. The woman who loved spending time with friends and family canceled plans at the last minute. The woman who always made sure she looked beautiful before stepping out of the house began spending most of her days on the couch or in bed without bothering to shower or get dressed. I still felt tremendous guilt about ignoring the obvious red flags. I was still angry at her for taking her own life. And I was still furious at myself for ignoring not just one, but three promptings. How different life would have been if only I had listened.

Anger mushroomed inside of me, pushing aside the feelings of love and happiness that had enveloped me moments earlier. I clenched my fists and my head throbbed. I glared at the smiling photograph of Krista and muttered, "I hate you."

As those words left my mouth, I felt dark and empty inside. I hadn't meant any of it. I loved Krista. I was more upset at myself than Krista for taking her life. I sat on the floor and leaned against the bed to calm down. Julianna's request that I wait until after the first anniversary of Krista's death to propose popped into my mind. I wanted Julianna and I to start our marriage on a solid foundation—one that could withstand the test of time, not only in this life, but throughout the eternities. To achieve that, I couldn't have feelings of anger or resentment toward another person—living or dead—standing in the way. I couldn't continue to beat myself up. I needed to find peace so I could focus my attention on a life and a future with Julianna—one that was unmarred by anger, guilt, and regret.

After collecting my emotions, I took another long look at Krista's graduation photo. I didn't know if taking it down would help me move forward but I figured it couldn't hurt. I removed it from the wall and held it tight to my chest for a long moment before placing it in the office closet next to the other photos.

Back in my room, I looked at the bare wall. I didn't feel any different but perhaps I was too emotionally spent to feel anything. I placed Julianna's engagement ring back in my sock drawer and hoped by the time I proposed I could find the peace I desperately sought. Julianna had received an answer to her prayers, and I needed answers to mine before I could propose.

•••

One Sunday morning, a few weeks after taking down the photo, I awoke from a nightmare, gasping for air. I kicked off the covers and sat up in bed. I had just relived Krista's suicide.

A sour feeling filled my stomach and bile rose in my throat. I swung my legs off the side of the bed, leaned forward, and pressed my forehead against my knees, waiting for the nausea to fade. In the meantime, I attempted to push the bloody details of her death from my mind. I thought of places and people that made me happy, like standing on the peak of Ben Lomond, a nearby mountain. I thought of Julianna and imagined her next to me.

The queasiness faded. The clock on my nightstand read 5:11 a.m. I stood. There was no point trying to go back to sleep. I was wide awake and worried that closing my eyes would trigger another nightmare.

Unfortunately, I was accustomed to flashbacks. In the months following Krista's death, I couldn't close my eyes without seeing her lifeless, bloodied body. Slowly the recollections had become less frequent, but when they hit, they were powerful. I hoped that meant I was healing.

As the sweat dried, I grabbed a blanket and headed to the front room. On the coffee table was a book, some magazines, and my scriptures. I tried reading all three but my mind was too rattled to concentrate. Instead, I got comfortable on the couch and again wished Julianna could keep me company. There'd be no need to exchange words. Just having her with me would be enough to tamp down the nerves and clear my head. But she wasn't there, so I was forced to push through it alone.

I found comfort in imagining our married life. I saw us going on morning runs, having children, and growing old together. It was enough to push most of the dread and darkness from my mind, and at some point, I nodded off.

I woke up to sunlight filling the house and a grumble in my stomach. The horror and dark feelings from earlier were mostly gone except a few fragments that stubbornly clung to my mind. I made scrambled eggs and toast, then showered, and dressed for church. Then I returned to the kitchen and looked at the fall colors as I washed the breakfast dishes. The leaves of the cottonwood, elm, and walnut trees next to my home were bright hues of yellow, red, and orange—a powerful reminder of the world's beauty.

While I stared at the colors and the leaves, my mind turned to Krista but instead of dwelling on her suicide, I thought about how much I missed and loved her. It was the first time since her death that I had thought about her without getting angry or sad. I reflected on the life we'd shared. It hadn't been perfect but it had been good and I was grateful.

"I'm sorry, Krista" I said. "I'm sorry for everything. Please forgive me for my inaction."

As the words left my mouth, a warm feeling engulfed my entire body. The peace I had been seeking for nearly a year had finally arrived. I could let Krista go. I also sensed she would approve of me starting a new life with Julianna. I closed my eyes and let the feeling wash over me. It was so warm and wonderful I wanted it to last forever. I didn't dare open my eyes for fear that the feeling would vanish.

I stood enjoying the quiet calm until the feeling faded away. I opened my eyes. The world outside the window hadn't changed. The leaves were still vibrant and the sky was blue. But internally I felt lighter, serene, with no guilt or regret. I was ready to move forward with Julianna.

CHAPTER TWENTY-FIVE

Julianna

I woke up on the morning of November 10, 2002 with a heavy, nervous feeling in my stomach. It was dark outside and I looked at the clock and groaned when I realized it was 4:30. I rolled over so my back was facing the clock and tried to go back to sleep, but my mind was too active, like honeybees buzzing in a flower garden. Finally, I just got out of bed.

Today was the first anniversary of Krista's death—a day I had been dreading and anticipating for weeks. I thought of the day as a final test for Abel and me. How would we handle such an emotionally-charged day? Would it draw us closer together or tear us apart? The anniversary fell on a Sunday, so we couldn't hide behind work, training runs or errands. The plan was to go to church and spend the day together.

I knew negative future fantasizing wasn't healthy but that hadn't stopped my imagination from dabbling in worst-case scenarios. In one, Abel spontaneously burst into tears and told me how much he missed Krista. In another he broke up with me after realizing Krista was the only woman he could ever love.

When I asked Abel how he planned to commemorate the day, he said he wanted to visit the cemetery and invited me to come. I worried that joining him would be intrusive, that I would be disrupting an intimate moment between Abel and his late wife. I had accepted that Krista would be part of our life and possibly play a role in the next one. I also knew she'd always hold a place in Abel's heart. That's why, as hard as it seemed, I was grateful to be spending the day with him while also learning more about Krista. By supporting Abel, I hoped I would know for sure if both of us were ready to start a new chapter.

I was able to quiet my thoughts until a few minutes before Abel was scheduled to pick me up. Would his eyes be red and puffy from crying when he arrived? Would he call at the last minute and say he didn't feel like going? It turns out, my worries were unfounded. Abel arrived on time and aside from some bags under his eyes that he said were from lack of sleep, he looked and acted normal. I felt a heaviness in the air as we drove to church, something I later learned that Abel was feeling, too. We both knew the significance of the day, even if it went unspoken.

I wondered whether someone might bring up Krista's name at church, if they might ask Abel how he's doing with the heaviness of the day. But her name was never mentioned. The meetings were uneventful and for that I was grateful. After the services, we changed and went back to Abel's home for lunch. Abel wasn't as chatty as usual, but otherwise it felt like a normal Sunday.

As we cleared the table, Abel checked his watch and said, "I'd like to wait a bit before heading to the cemetery."

"Whatever you want," I said even though I'd hoped we'd go to the cemetery sooner rather than later as I was anxious to see how this would play out, but it was Abel's day. After washing the dishes, we ended up on the couch. Abel rested his head on my lap and closed his eyes. I brushed his hair with my fingers and for a long while we sat in silence, each lost in our individual worlds.

I don't know how long we sat like that but it was late afternoon when Abel opened his eyes and said, "I'm ready to go."

As we put on our coats, I realized that we didn't have flowers or something else to pay respects. The thought of bringing something had crossed my mind several times that week but I wasn't sure it was my place to do so and assumed Abel would have flowers or some other token but his hands were empty.

"Are you bringing flowers or something else?" I asked, as Abel opened the side door of the house.

Abel paused, then shook his head. "No," he said, then added "Just us."

We made the short drive, like so much of our day, in silence. When our relationship first blossomed, silence bothered me. But after six months together, I had learned that sometimes we each needed silence to sort out our feelings.

The cemetery where Krista was laid to rest is a ten-acre grassy hill with another twenty acres available for expansion nearby. It had a gravel road and trees staked to the ground. Without the sign at the entrance, the cemetery could be easily mistaken for a park.

Abel parked the car at the top of the hill. He opened my car door then gave my hand a squeeze as if to say "Are you ready for this?" I squeezed his hand back letting him know I was. He guided me past rows of in-ground headstones to Krista's final resting place, near the top of the hill—high enough that I could see all the way to the Great Salt Lake.

Krista's headstone was identical to the other headstones we'd passed with one exception: this one had two names on it. I hadn't known that Krista and Hope shared the same grave. I'd assumed they were buried next to each other. A wide-mouth canning jar brimming with a bouquet of chrysanthemums was placed next to their headstone. The orange and yellow flowers looked fresh, bright and alive in stark contrast to the cemetery's dead, matted grass and I caught a whiff of their earthy scent.

"My mom's been here," Abel said motioning to the jar.

I noted empty plots on either side of their headstone and remembered Abel mentioning months earlier that he had a plot next to Krista. For the first time it struck me that Abel might want to be buried next to them. We had focused so much time and energy into creating and sustaining our relationship that it never occurred to me to ask Abel where he wanted to be buried or where I wanted my final resting place to be. I made a mental note to have that conversation with Abel at a later date.

I returned my attention to Abel. There were no tears, but he had a distant look in his eyes and the corners of his mouth seemed pulled down by invisible weights, giving his face a sad, forlorn look. Unsure what to do or say I took Abel's hand and focused my attention on the view to the west, on the setting sun, the mountains, and the Great Salt Lake whose waters were the color of butternut squash. I admired the sight until I heard the crunch of tires on gravel. Two cars made their way along the road and parked behind Abel's car. A couple got out of one car and a lone traveler emerged from the other. I recognized the couple as Ryan and Suzie—Abel and Krista's friends. I didn't know the other woman but Abel introduced her as Sylvia, his former boss from when he and Krista worked at the college writing center.

I listened as the four of them caught up on life and shared memories of Krista. There were stories from working in the college writing center together, from a school trip to Arizona, a vacation to Southern Utah, and funny, witty remarks she'd made. I didn't mind the stories but felt like I was on the outside of an inside joke. It was a little uncomfortable but mostly served as a reminder that there was a part of Abel's life that he had shared with someone else and though I'd get occasional glimpses into his past, it was something that I would never fully be part of. I wondered how long it would take the two of us to reach a point where we'd have our own memories, traditions, and inside jokes.

As the last of the sun dipped behind the mountains, we all headed toward our cars.

"Thanks for coming," Abel said, taking my hand as we drove home. "I know the day wasn't easy for you."

"I don't think it was easy for anyone," I said.

While we were driving back to Abel's house, it occurred to me that Abel might want to visit the cemetery every November tenth, and perhaps other days like Krista's birthday or their wedding anniversary. I'd support him in those visits, but one trip to the cemetery was enough for me. After a quick dinner, Abel dropped me off at my apartment and said he'd see me at five the next morning for our run.

As I got into bed, I felt confident that Abel was ready to start the next chapter of his life. Even though there were unanswered questions, like how often he would visit the cemetery or what our relationship would look like in the next life, I didn't dwell on them. Instead, I focused on the progress we'd made over the last six months and wondered how soon Abel would ask me to marry him.

CHAPTER TWENTY-SIX

Abel

The morning after the first anniversary of Krista's death, I woke up feeling like Superman. Bulletproof. Invincible. Powerful. Life could throw any obstacle at me, and I'd figure out a way to overcome it.

I hadn't expected to feel that way considering the powerful emotions of the previous day. But as I contemplated the sensation of invincibility on the drive to work, I realized I had just mentally, emotionally, physically, and spiritually survived the hardest year of my life. It hadn't been a smooth ride, but through a combination of perseverance, guidance from above, and a little luck, I had not only endured, but come out stronger. My heart had been smashed to pieces, but I had rebuilt a bigger and tougher version of it. My old life was destroyed, but I had built the foundation of a new one. Though I didn't believe my journey was over, I felt that I had conquered the most difficult part of it.

Along with the invincibility came new mental acuity. It was as if some innocence had been ripped away and replaced with insight and understanding that can only be achieved through experience. Losing Krista and Hope made me look at the world and the people I knew differently. Life could change at any moment, and the time we spent with those we loved was precious and fragile. I had been fortunate to find love a second time and wasn't going to let that opportunity go to waste so I started planning how I'd propose to Julianna.

I considered asking her after a long Saturday run, at my home, or out on Antelope Island where we had our first good date. I ended up rejecting those ideas because I couldn't think of a way to make the moment memorable. I didn't want to simply get down on my knees. I wanted to provide an experience that would actually mean something for both of us.

My proposal to Krista was something she had relished. I did it on a trip to Casper, Wyoming, to visit family. When we approached Independence Rock, I stopped and told Krista I needed to stretch my legs and invited her to climb the turtle-shell-shaped rock with me. Alone at the top, we were greeted with sweeping views of the Wyoming prairie. I got down on one knee and proposed. Krista said "Yes!" She later told me she appreciated the unique setting along with the irony of joining our lives in a place where Independence was part of the name. I wanted Julianna to feel the same excitement whenever she talked about or remembered her proposal.

Finally, I decided that once it snowed, I'd write a big message in the fields behind my parents' home. All I needed for that was a couple inches of fresh powder. Usually, the first snow came around Thanksgiving, but as that holiday came and went, the ground was barren and brown and there was no snow in the forecast. I scrapped those plans, unsure what to do, but feeling I needed to ask her soon.

One evening soon after Thanksgiving, our dinner conversation shifted to our first date.

"I can't believe we turned something so awful into something so beautiful," I said as I remembered the horrified look on Julianna's face when I told her I was widowed.

"I can still feel that chicken sliding down my throat like a rock," Julianna said. "It's hard to believe everything worked out."

"There were a lot of small miracles along the way," I said. "I still owe your dad one for suggesting you go out with me again."

"Don't forget that Brian never came to church with me."

"Or that your marathon photo was on the front of the sports page."

"And my apartment stayed in the ward when the boundaries were redrawn."

"Makes you wonder if things would have turned out differently if any one of those miracles hadn't happened," I said.

"Some of those moments didn't seem like miracles at the time," Julianna said. "I still have no idea what my dad was thinking when he said to give you a second chance."

"I'm glad he said something," I said, "because after that awful first date, miracles were the only thing that would have gotten us back together." As I spoke those words, a thought popped into my head and I realized how I was going to propose. "I still feel awful that our first date didn't go as planned," I said. "I need to make it up to you. Why don't we take a drive to Logan on Saturday and have lunch at the Bluebird?"

"That's sweet," Julianna replied, "but you don't have to do that."

"Wouldn't it be nice to have some good memories of Logan for a change?"

Julianna laughed, "Yes, it would."

"Then let's plan on it. After our run Saturday morning, we'll clean up, and spend the day there."

Julianna agreed. Inside, I was excited as my plan fell into place.

For the rest of the week, my thoughts were consumed by the proposal. The one thing I struggled with was where in Logan to pop the question. Our mutual dislike of public proposals meant that the Bluebird was out. Logan had a beautiful Latter-day Saint temple, but considering that was the temple where Krista and I were sealed, proposing on those well-manicured grounds wasn't an option. In the end, I decided that Logan Canyon was both private and beautiful, and would be the perfect place to ask Julianna to marry me.

The days dragged by, and our nine-mile Saturday morning run seemed to last forever. When it finally ended, I hurried home to shower, excited for the rest of the day to unfold. After cleaning up, I took the ring out of my sock drawer and took a long look at it. A nervous flutter filled my stomach. Even though I was confident Julianna would say yes, there was always a small chance she would say no. I put the ring in my pocket and told myself that no matter what she decided, I would respect her choice.

Julianna arrived a few minutes later. Instead of throwing her hair back in a ponytail like she normally did on Saturdays, she had curled her hair, and it reminded me of the very first time I saw her at church. She looked gorgeous. My finger traced the outline of the ring in my pocket, and it took every ounce of strength not to propose on the spot.

On the drive to Logan, I did my best to act normal and hoped I wasn't giving away some nonverbal clues that something was up. At the Bluebird, as we were waiting to be seated, I leaned close to Julianna and said, "Last time we ate here, I dropped the widower bomb on you."

Julianna smiled. "I'm glad we were able to move past that."

"Me too," I said. "I promise not to drop any bombs on you during this meal."

We both chuckled. It felt good to turn that horrible moment into something we could laugh about.

Because I was nervous, I wasn't really hungry but ate anyway, trying to focus my mind on other things. When the meal was over, we took a drive up the canyon. It had been a decade since I was last there, and I realized that I didn't know where, exactly, in the canyon I was going to ask for her hand in marriage. Finally, I spotted some parking spots near a trailhead. There weren't any other cars in the parking lot, and it appeared we had this tiny corner of the canyon all to ourselves.

Most of the canyon was in shadow, and with several inches of snow on the ground, it was much colder than in Logan. It didn't take long to realize neither of us were dressed for the cold. If I was going to propose, it would have to be soon or I'd need to find a warmer place to pop the question. We walked along the trail. Once the road was out of sight, I took one last look around to make sure we were alone.

"Stand right there," I said.

"Okay," Julianna said, giving me a puzzled look.

I spaced myself out so I was an arm length from her and walked around her in a circle several times.

"What am I doing?" I asked

"You're walking in circles," she said.

"That's a good guess, but I'm actually making you the center of my universe."

Julianna smiled. "That's sweet."

"But I don't just want to be in your orbit," I said. "I want to merge our two lives and become one."

I took the ring from my pocket and knelt in the snow in front of her.

"Julianna, will you marry me and be my wife forever?"

Julianna's eyes grew wide as a look of surprise filled her face. Then her lips parted into the biggest smile I'd ever seen. It's an image that is seared in my mind and something I'll never forget. I knew what her answer would be before the words left her mouth.

"Yes! Yes! Yes!" Julianna said.

She flung her arms around me, and we kissed over and over and over again.

I held out the ring that was still clutched tightly between my thumb and index finger. "This is part of the deal," I said.

She flashed another big smile.

"It's just what I wanted!" she squealed.

I slid the ring on her finger. We kissed again and enjoyed the moment until the cold ate through our clothing. Then we walked back to the car holding hands.

It was time to tell everyone that we were engaged.

CHAPTER TWENTY-SEVEN

Julianna

I'm engaged! I'm engaged! I'm engaged!

I looked at the ring on my finger still shocked that Abel popped the question. We had been talking about marriage, but for some reason I hadn't expected Abel to propose as part of an "impromptu" trip to Logan. It was a wonderful surprise. It felt almost like a dream; that I'd wake up any moment. But it wasn't a dream, it was real! I was ecstatic at the thought of spending the rest of my life and eternity with Abel and I couldn't wait to start our life together.

"When do you want to tell everyone?" Abel asked as we drove back to Ogden.

His question brought me out of my happy reverie.

"I should probably call my parents first." I said and fished my cell phone out of the cup holder.

"You don't want to tell them in person?"

"I do, but I should probably give them a heads-up," I said. I dialed the home line then put my phone on speaker so Abel could hear. I was excited and nervous to tell them the news.

My mom answered and I said, "I need to talk with both you and dad."

I hoped the excitement in my voice wouldn't spoil the surprise.

My mom must not have caught the anticipation or maybe she mistook it for agitation because she said, "Is everything okay, Julie?"

"Just get dad," I said doing my best to sound normal.

When they were both on the line, I announced "Abel asked me to marry him!"

There was silence then my dad said, "Well, what did you say?"

"I said yes, of course."

Abel burst into laughter and squeezed my hand.

"Congratulations," my dad said. "That's wonderful."

In the background I heard my mom pass the news to my sisters followed by their excited chatter. I told them briefly about the proposal then said the two of us would stop by later that evening.

After I hung up Abel said, "We should probably tell my family next."

The idea of calling Abel's family tempered my enthusiasm. I assumed they'd be happy for us, but what if they thought Abel was moving on too fast or someone was upset that he was getting engaged? I couldn't control their reactions, but I also didn't want anyone else's feelings sabotaging our moment.

As if sensing my concern Abel took my hand. "If you want, we can go to the ward Christmas dinner first."

In all the excitement, I had forgotten about the dinner. We planned to attend but that was before Abel popped the question. I looked at the ring on my finger. I wanted to go to the dinner. The ward had been nothing but supportive of our relationship but Abel's family should know about the engagement first.

"Let's tell your family," I said.

Abel gave my hand a squeeze. "No matter what happens, it will be okay."

As Abel gathered his family in the kitchen, concerns about negative reactions returned. This wasn't how I dreamed I would feel about sharing the news with my fiancé's family. I had always expected an engagement would make everyone happy. Then again, I never imagined myself marrying a widower. Once everyone was in the kitchen, I took Abel's hand and said a quick prayer that the announcement would be well received.

With a big smile, Abel said, "I asked Julianna to marry me, and she said yes."

There was silence and I took in a breath. Were they surprised? Shocked? Upset?

Abel's grandmother broke the silence. "It's Pearl Harbor Day," she said.

It was an odd thing to say and I wasn't sure what to make of it. His grandmother's words were quickly followed by "Congratulations, that's wonderful news. I'm excited for the two of you."

After I had time to sort through my feelings, his grandmother's reaction made sense. December 7th was a day that carried a lot of significance for her generation.

Abel's brother and sister broke into smiles and everyone offered their congratulations. They didn't seem as excited as my family but I tried to give them the benefit of the doubt. Maybe this was as happy as Abel's family got. I looked at Abel in an attempt to read his reaction. He still had a big smile on his face and didn't seem concerned about his family's response. I relaxed and chided myself for getting worked up.

At some point there was a lull in the conversation and then Abel's mom spoke. Since Abel broken the news, she'd been standing to one side of the room with a perplexed look on her face and hadn't said anything.

"I had a dream about Krista last night," she said.

Her words brought an immediate hush to the room. Instantly the elation I felt was replaced by a wave of nausea. Krista's name was the last thing I wanted to hear.

Abel squeezed my hand as if telling me not to worry.

"In my dream I saw Krista and she was happy," Abel's mom continued. "Krista was smiling and her face was radiant and looked like it had sparkles on it. It was like she was trying to tell me that she was happy and everything was okay with her."

I was speechless. Why was she sharing this information *now*? This was Abel's and my moment to celebrate. Why did she feel the need to make Krista part of it? I felt a concoction of anger, dejection, and despair well up inside me. *Couldn't this moment just be about us? Why is she more concerned about the dead than the living?*

As if sensing my feelings, Abel gave my hand a second squeeze. He stared at the floor; his jaw clenched. I tensed, unsure what to do or say. Finally, he said, "We're going to head to the ward dinner."

I was surprised by his impromptu announcement but relieved that Abel wanted to leave. I couldn't stay any longer. My day wasn't ruined but it was certainly marred. I kept my mouth shut so I wouldn't say something I'd regret.

We excused ourselves and hurried to the car.

"I'm sorry about that," Abel said as he opened my door. "I don't know why my mom felt the need to share her dream."

"I just wanted the day to be about us," I said. "Sometimes I wish that your old life wouldn't overlap with your new one."

"I'm doing my best to keep them separate."

"It's not you I'm worried about," I replied. "It's everyone else."

"We can't control what others say or how they react," Abel said. "Instead of dwelling on what just happened, let's focus on the future."

Even though Abel was right, his words did little to ease the resentment and frustration I felt. I didn't understand the need to talk about the dead when her son had just announced his engagement.

Abel started the car and said, "Do you still want to go to the ward dinner?"

I needed some time before seeing my parents. The last thing I wanted was to arrive sad or angry. "Yes," I said. "Let's go."

"Are you sure?"

I nodded.

On the drive to the church Abel said "Do you want to say anything about our engagement to anyone at church?"

I wanted to tell everyone about the news but after what happened with Abel's family, I was hesitant. What if someone at the dinner had a negative reaction to the news. "Let's keep it to ourselves."

"You sure?"

"If someone sees the ring and asks, we tell them," I said. "Let's see how things play out."

When we arrived at the party, the parking lot was nearly full. Though these types of activities are typically well attended, I was surprised by the number of cars. As I waited for Abel to open my door, a couple with three young children in tow hurried toward the building. They opened the doors, spilling warm, yellow light into the cold, dark air. I caught a glimpse of families sitting at tables eating. The church looked warm, inviting, and happy and I couldn't wait to join the festivities.

Inside there were four long rows of tables covered in butcher paper. The air smelled of roast beef and freshly baked rolls. Most of the seats were already taken but we found some space at a table where the married couples who didn't have any children had congregated. It was hard not to say anything about the ring on my finger. I wanted to share our news with everyone but managed to focus on the food and the conversation.

Halfway through the meal the woman sitting across from me looked at my left hand and did a double take. Her eyes grew wide.

"Is that an engagement ring?" she said.

My body tensed as I nodded. I didn't know the woman well. Did she know Krista? Would the news upset her?

"When did that happen?" she said, her voice tinged with excitement.

"This afternoon," I said.

"Today?"

"A few hours ago."

She let out a delighted squeal and then asked to see my ring. I let out a breath, exorcizing the built-up tension of the last few seconds. As I held out my hand, her husband leaned over and asked what was going on.

"Julianna and Abel are engaged!" she said.

"Really? Congratulations!" he said.

The woman sitting next to him looked over and asked what the excitement was about. The man pointed at the two of us and though I couldn't hear his words, I could read his lips as he shared the news with her. The woman smiled, elbowed her husband and then told him. I watched as the news was passed down the table.

Abel, who had been watching too, smiled and squeezed my hand. He leaned in close and said, "I guess everyone's going to know before the party's over," he said.

Through the rest of the dinner, people came to our table and congratulated us on our engagement. At some point someone got on the stage, tapped the microphone, and announced the news to everyone. That was followed by cheers and applause and even more people came over to share their congratulations. I repeated the story of Abel's proposal over and over and over again, showing off my new ring at every opportunity. I was thrilled that the same congregation that had embraced Abel and Krista's relationship, was just as accepting and excited about ours.

Before the party ended, we excused ourselves so we could officially celebrate with my family. It was going to be a long, late night but I was on cloud nine. My thoughts were on picking a wedding day and how soon we could become husband and wife.

"We still haven't decided where to live after getting married," Abel said. "What if I sold my house and we lived somewhere else?"

I was happy at the news but wasn't sure what to say. We had discussed the issue a few months earlier but had never decided where we would live. Now that we were engaged, we had to make a decision soon.

"Where do you want to live?" I asked.

"Somewhere that would split the distance between our jobs. Somewhere like Farmington or Bountiful."

He motioned out the window and I realized we were driving through the exact area he was talking about.

"What if you lose money on your house?"

Abel shrugged. "Seems like a small price to pay if it means we can start our wedding in a home and a community without ties to the past."

I liked the idea but didn't say anything. Instead, I took Abel's hand in mine. In the distance I could see the Bountiful Temple on the mountain. It was lit with white lights and reminded me of a bright planet in the midst of a starry sky. As I took one last look at the temple, I realized that the words, dreams, or actions of others couldn't stop Abel and me from tying the knot. The only people who could stop us from reaching that destination together were each other. With that thought I pushed aside the hurt and began thinking how soon we could make our dream become reality.

CHAPTER TWENTY-EIGHT

Abel

In early January, I put my house on the market hoping to find a buyer before February 28, our wedding day. There were many reasons not to sell: a mortgage payment that was cheaper than renting, the money and time I had sunk into fixing it, and the fact that selling it a year after buying meant I would probably take a significant loss. Keeping the property would allow us to pay off Julianna's student loans and our cars faster and make it easier to start a nest egg. But the question I kept coming back to was: What's best for mine and Julianna's marriage? Was it staying in Ogden or starting a new life somewhere else?

The area I lived in was dense with memories of my life with Krista. And even though she had never lived in the home, buying and fixing it up so she could live close to her grandmother and my family had been Krista's dream—not mine. Ultimately, I decided that I wanted a fresh start with Julianna and selling the house was the best way to achieve that, even if it meant our finances would be tight for a few years. In my mind, that was a small price to pay for a strong foundation on which to build our marriage.

To my surprise, the house sold within weeks of putting it on the market. I made an agreement with the buyer to stay in the home until the end of February, giving Julianna and I enough time to find a new place before our wedding day.

With the house sold, we spent our evenings searching for apartments. We looked at places from Layton to Bountiful—far enough away from the memories of my past life but close enough that our commutes to work would be bearable. We ended up signing a month-to-month lease on a one-bedroom, basement apartment of a large home four miles south of the Bountiful Temple. The apartment was smaller than Julianna's one-bedroom apartment but it was affordable. On the drive back to Ogden after signing the paperwork and paying the deposit, we were both happy to have a place we could soon call ours.

As we got on the freeway, Julianna said, "What are we going to do with our stuff?"

In the excitement about finding a new place I hadn't thought about combining our possessions. When Krista and I married, we started with nothing. Our couch, bed, and table were hand-me-downs from our families and friends. We added a few things over the years but hadn't accumulated much. Still, adding those items with things from Julianna's apartment meant two kitchen tables, two couches, two beds, two sets of dishes. Two of just about everything. It couldn't all come with us.

"Guess we'll have to give some things away," I said.

"I'd prefer to keep my couch," she said.

Neither her couch nor mine were that comfortable but hers was long enough that I could lie on it and fit my six-foot-three frame without touching either end. Though mine wasn't nearly as long, there were memories of Krista attached to the couch—snuggling in one corner watching a movie or sitting with Krista's legs on my lap while we both did homework or read. Could I give up something that held fond memories? I asked myself if holding on to the couch would hurt or strengthen my marriage to Julianna and realized I didn't want it to come between us.

"That's fine," I said. "Do you think it will fit in our new place?"

"I think so."

"I have a nicer kitchen table," I said. "And matching chairs to go with it."

Out of all our worldly possessions, the oak kitchen table and chairs were the nicest pieces of furniture Krista and I owned. I liked them not only because they were good looking, but because of the memories associated with finding them. The kitchen table had been an inexpensive, accidental find at a scratch-and-dent sale right after moving to our second apartment. The six matching chairs had come a week later when a neighbor had a yard sale. It was the serendipitous coming together of the chairs and table that made them meaningful. I smiled as the memories replayed in my mind.

"I guess," Julianna said.

"You don't sound enthusiastic about keeping it." I didn't think Julianna knew the story of the table and chairs but maybe I had mentioned it. Was that the reason she didn't want to keep them?

"It's kind of big for the space," she said.

I debated whether to tell Julianna the story behind the table and the chairs but decided against it. Whatever furniture or other possessions we kept, I wanted it to be for practical reasons—not emotional ones. "It's better than your table," I said. "It's more than we need now but won't it be nice to have a big table once a couple of kids come along?"

"You're right. We'll make it work," she said.

We went through a few other items. By the time we arrived in Ogden, we had made a decision about every big item except the bed.

"We can keep my bed," I said. "Your bed isn't big enough for both of us."

"I'm not sleeping in the same bed you and Krista shared." Her words sounded forceful. Maybe she felt they sounded too strong because she followed up with. "I'm fine with Krista's table and a few other things but our bed needs to be something that belongs only to us."

Her words gave me pause. I hadn't thought about that.

"That's fine," I said. "But what's your solution?"

"We can buy a new mattress. We can use that basic metal frame that comes with it. I know that we're trying to save money and pay off debt but our bed needs to be the one thing that's ours."

I opened my mouth to say something about the expense of a new mattress but put myself in Julianna's shoes. If she was the one who was widowed, how would I feel about sleeping in the bed that she had shared with her husband? It wasn't very appealing.

Julianna continued, "At the lab I've seen the evidence that comes back from hotels and bedrooms. You wouldn't believe the various body fluids we find on comforters and mattresses. There was this one blanket—"

"I get the point," I said. "We'll buy a new mattress."

"Thanks," Julianna said. She reached for my hand, sliding her fingers between mine. "It's important to have at least one thing that only we shared."

"Give it time. One day we'll own lots of things that will feel like ours." I said.

After I got home and looked at the couch, table, and other items we had discussed I realized we hadn't addressed Krista's things. Twelve cardboard boxes that contained her papers, letters, journals, photographs, and other items were still stacked in the corner of my office, largely untouched since I moved into the home. Several times I'd attempted to sort through the contents but within minutes of opening a box, I'd be in tears from reliving the life that Krista and I had planned. But with my marriage to Julianna less than a month away, I knew I needed to get cracking. Just thinking about reopening those boxes—and my old wounds—made my heart feel heavy.

The boxes couldn't come with me, and not just because of the space constraints. The real issue was what the contents represented: my life and marriage to Krista. It didn't feel right taking so much of my past with me, but it didn't feel right throwing everything away either. There had to be a solution, a compromise that both Julianna and I would feel good about, but tonight I wasn't in the right mindset to put much thought into it. Instead, I closed the office door knowing the issue would soon be resolved.

•••

We opened the boxes together two weeks later. A few days before sorting through them I had told Julianna my plans and asked if she wanted to be part of it. She had agreed though she seemed hesitant and I worried how the experience would turn out. Years later I would learn that she wanted to be supportive and was curious about what the boxes contained. At the same time, she worried how we would both emotionally handle digging through my past life.

We stood in the doorway to the office and took a long look at the pile of boxes like they were ancient, mysterious objects. Finally, I took the top box and put it on the floor.

"I'm going to sort everything into two piles," I said. "One to keep and one to throw away. You can help me decide, if you want."

Julianna took a seat on the floor next to me. "It's not my place to decide," she said. "These are your things. What to keep is up to you."

I took a deep breath. Did I have the strength to make these decisions? Had I made the right decision to invite Julianna to be part of this moment or would her presence sway me to dispose of things I wasn't ready to part with? There was only one way to find out.

The top item in the first box was a photo album. I didn't have to open it up to know that it contained photos of our engagement and wedding. I picked it up and put it in the space I had designated to keep things.

"What's this?" Julianna said.

"Photos," I said then added, "Mostly wedding pictures."

Julianna's eyes wandered over the cover and I could tell curiosity was getting the best of her.

"You can look at it if you want," I said.

Julianna's finger traced the edges of the album before pushing it away.

"What else is in the box?" she said.

I removed the scrapbook of Hope's brief life—the one my mom had made—and placed it in the keep pile.

"You don't have any photos of Hope up," Julianna said.

"I know."

"You can put a photo of her up in our apartment, if you want," Julianna said.

My stomach tightened. "Thanks, but that's not necessary."

"Really. It's fine. I wouldn't mind."

"No," I said putting enough force in my voice to deter the subject further.

"Okay," Julianna said holding up her hands in mock surrender.

I reached into the box and pulled out a pile of papers. It was a mix of Krista's essays, poetry, and some short fiction. I flipped through them, trying to figure out what to keep and what to toss. The problem was I wanted to keep everything. Each paper evoked memories of poetry readings, completing assignments at the last minute at the computer lab, doing research at the library late into the night, or working at the university's writing center together. Memories came at a furious pace and it felt like I was reliving parts of my life all over again.

"Are you alright?" Julianna asked.

Her words yanked me back to the present.

"I'm fine," I said pushing the memories to the side. It was mostly true. Emotions were churning inside me but they weren't as strong or powerful as I thought they'd be. As I placed the papers in the "keep" pile, I realized the feelings weren't as strong because I no longer felt married to Krista. I still loved her, but she was not the pinnacle of my thoughts. That place had been given to Julianna. As a result of that switch, there was enough emotional separation that looking through the contents of that life was like remembering good times with friends.

I returned my attention to the box. In the bottom was a pile of cassette tapes. I recognized them, too. One day before a trip to Wyoming to visit my family, Krista had the idea of bringing a cassette recorder to help pass the time. When we got bored, we'd turn on the recorder and talk about whatever was on our minds. We had so much fun making that first recording that it became something we did every time we took a long trip together. There were ten tapes in the bottom of the box, each one labeled with different places we had traveled—Denver, Colorado; St. George, Utah; Casper, Wyoming; Wendover, Nevada; Pocatello, Idaho. Just seeing the tapes and their destination was enough to make me relive each trip in a matter of seconds. I stacked the tapes in the "keep" pile because they contained recordings of Krista's voice.

I glanced up at Julianna. She looked to the "keep" pile then at unopened pile of boxes as if to note I hadn't put anything in the "toss" pile.

"I'm not keeping everything," I said, not sure how to explain that tossing items from the boxes was like throwing away part of my life. I knew that memories alone weren't reason enough to keep something, but there had to be some way to set aside my emotions and look at them more rationally.

I leafed through the pile of papers and found a poem Krista had written.

Midwestern Philosophy

I spent the summer in
Omaha, Nebraska with my cousins
who are completely unrelated
to anyone who ever knew anything.
Other things to consider about Omaha,
are the straight highways
and the four, I guess you'd call
them farm hands,
who stood with zig-zag boot legs
pissing a quadri-stream of pride
onto the shell of a dead turtle
in the ditch by the road.
And I wondered as we sped passed
if that late lump of reptile was
the one that turned aside for nothing,
as it parted the yellow grass.
It was something to consider—
no ordinary dying going on in Omaha;
highways running straight into the
North Platte without slowing down.

It had been years since I had read it, but remembered Krista drafting it out on a piece of scrap paper as we drove back to Utah after spending a long weekend with my family who lived in Casper, Wyoming at the time. As we drove the two-lane highway that connects Casper to Rawlins, we slowed for a truck that was parked off to the side of the road. Next to the truck four cowboys, wearing Stetsons and cowboy boots, stood in a line relieving themselves. One of the cowboys waved as we sped past. Krista and I had burst into laughter at the sight.

"I'm going to turn that moment into a poem," she said when our laughter had died down and spent the next hour writing her first draft. Reading that poem brought back fond memories and also gave me an idea: The things I'd keep were those that would best show who Krista was. It wasn't something that would be shown through trinkets, clothing, or other worldly possessions but through her poetry, photos, and journals. The things I'd keep would provide insights about her personality, our relationship, and how she viewed the world. It made the decision of what to keep and what to toss a lot easier.

I opened the second box. Krista's jewelry box was on top. The only thing I wanted to keep was my wedding band and her wedding ring. I put the symbols of our marriage on top of the papers, set the jewelry box in the "toss" pile, and made a mental note to ask my sisters if they wanted any of the contents before I disposed of it.

After that, the sorting went faster and before long the "toss" pile outweighed the "keep" pile. As I put things into the two piles, Julianna asked me questions about items I was keeping or discarding.

"What's this?" Julianna asked lifting a lid off the shoebox I had put in the keep pile.

"Letters Krista wrote to me on my mission," I said.

"There's a lot of them."

"She wrote every week."

Julianna put the lid back on the shoebox then picked up a photo album. "Can I look?" she asked.

"If you want," I said.

As Julianna looked through the album, I glanced at the photos and recognized them from the first year of our married life together.

"Where was this photo taken?" Julianna pointed at a photo of Krista and I standing by a large cactus.

"Tucson," I said. "School-sponsored trip to the University of Arizona."

"Were you married then?"

"Newlyweds," I answered. "Married two or three months at the time."

She flipped a few more pages. "You graduated together?"

There were two pages of Krista and I standing outside in black caps and gowns—photos my mom took after the graduation ceremony. Had I not told her that we graduated at the same time? She knew we had gone to school together and both had liberal arts degrees but the graduation part must not have come out. The photos were a reminder that I was still trying to figure out the right balance of when to talk about my life and marriage to Krista and when to keep my mouth shut. Maybe sorting through the boxes was a good way for her to learn more without feeling like I was caught up in the past.

"We did," I said. "That took place about six months after we were married."

She turned the page. There were photos of a friend and I sitting in lawn chairs waiting for tickets for the new Star Wars movie and some of the two of us taking a hike in the mountains east of Ogden. She didn't ask any questions this time but took her time looking at the pictures. Sometimes I glanced at the photos and momentarily relived those moments. Even though the photos were only two or three years old, they felt like a lifetime ago.

Julianna closed the album and placed it atop the keep pile. I placed a box of Krista's clothing in the toss pile.

"You're getting rid of lots of stuff."

"I can move everything to the keep pile if you want."

"That's not what I meant," Julianna said elbowing me. "I just don't want you to regret throwing anything away."

"You mean getting rid of stuff that I don't want to toss because you're in the same room?"

"Something like that."

My mind flashed back to Krista's poem. "I'm keeping what's really important."

It took another hour to finish. What I kept filled two large packing boxes. They contained photos of our life together, letters we exchanged while I was on my mission, Krista's journal, poetry and short stories, the cassette tapes of our trips, her college diploma, our marriage certificate and other legal documents. It was enough to showcase our relationship, and should anyone look at the contents, give a good idea about Krista, her interests, and her personality. Everything else filled four black trash bags. I taped the boxes shut, sat on the floor, and leaned against the wall. I hadn't cried but the task of sorting, prioritizing, and tossing had been emotionally draining.

Julianna sat next to me and leaned her head on my shoulder.

"I'm glad that's over," I said.

"Me too," Julianna said.

"You're sure you're okay with taking these two boxes to our new place?"

"Yes," she said. "I am."

These two boxes would go with Julianna and I to our new apartment where they would be put in the corner of our bedroom closet. As we moved from one apartment to another, to our first home, then to another, these two boxes came with us. They would find places in storage rooms and closets, spare bedrooms and garages but would always have a place wherever we lived.

PART THREE
Married Life

CHAPTER TWENTY-NINE

Julianna

I woke up with Abel's arm wrapped around my waist. Bright morning light filtered in through the window well. I closed my eyes and enjoyed the press of Abel's body against mine. Abel stirred and nuzzled his face into my hair. "Morning, love," he said, then, "What time is it?"

The clock on the nightstand read 7:30. We didn't have to get up and going until eight. I gave his arm a squeeze and said, "We have thirty more minutes."

"Good," Abel said. "I'm tired."

It took only a moment for Abel to fall back asleep. I enjoyed his warm, rhythmic breath on my neck. I was too awake to sleep, but wanted the moment to last as long as possible.

I loved being married to Abel. I loved lying next to him on Sunday mornings. I loved the wonderful, quiet life we'd built in Bountiful. In the three months since tying the knot, we'd found new running routes, delicious restaurants, and a bookstore. We'd enjoyed attending a new ward where the only thing anyone really knew was that we were newlyweds.

The thirty minutes in Abel's arms passed quickly. After some playful groaning about getting up, we got out of bed, showered, and dressed for church. After the services, a member of the bishopric approached us. After some small talk, he said, "I'd like to extend to you an opportunity to speak in church."

My stomach tightened. The request didn't come as a complete surprise. In Latter-day Saint services, members of the congregation deliver most of the sermons and lessons. One reason new move-ins are asked to speak is because it gives the rest of the congregation a chance to get to know them better.

"Of course," Abel said. "Is there something you'd like us to talk about?"

I can't remember the assigned topic. It might have been following the Spirit or receiving answers to prayers, but I remember feeling that I should share my story and experience about dating and marrying Abel. This surprised me. Bountiful was our chance to start fresh and focus on building a new life together. Sharing something so deeply personal in front of a new congregation, most of whom were strangers, seemed to negate the main reason we had moved.

We had two weeks to prepare. A few days after receiving the assignment, Abel and I sat down to draft our talks. Still not wanting to share anything personal, I tried writing about something else, but my mind went blank. No matter how hard I tried, I couldn't put any thoughts together. The words only flowed when I finally gave in and wrote about my experience dating and falling in love with Abel. I followed the impression and wrote a condensed version of my and Abel's story.

When the Sunday of our talk arrived, anxiety nearly got the best of me. I would have felt nervous about speaking regardless of the topic. Speaking in front of people was never something I had enjoyed. However, sharing such a personal story added an extra layer of unease. Abel, who enjoyed public speaking, appeared more nervous than usual.

"I can't believe I'm going to talk about us," I said as we drove to church.

Abel squeezed my hand. "Maybe someone needs to hear our story," he said.

Who needs to hear this message? I thought. Talks about tithing, reading scriptures, or Christ I could understand. A talk about dating and marrying a widower given to a congregation composed of married couples and children seemed odd.

The service passed quickly, and then it was my turn to speak. I stood in front of the congregation and shared my story. I told them about our awful first date, my concern about dating a young widower, receiving answers to my prayers, and deciding to move forward with the relationship despite not knowing how things might turn out in the next life. I finished my talk and sat next to Abel, relieved it was over. As the congregation sang a hymn, I hoped that despite sharing such a personal message, Abel and I could continue building our own quiet life together in Bountiful. After the hymn, Abel shared his words and the services ended.

To my astonishment, ten women approached me after the meeting. Several were in tears.

"Thank you for telling your story," one woman said.

"We never discuss this topic in church," another told me. "I'm so glad you shared your experience."

A third said, "Your talk answered questions I've had about eternal marriage and families."

Some of them had questions and wanted to hear more about my journey. While talking with them, I noticed a woman standing on the outskirts of the group. She looked to be in her early to mid-forties. Occasionally we made eye contact, and she smiled each time our eyes met. She waited patiently until the other women left, then took my hand in hers and said, "I'm a second wife too."

It took a moment for her words to sink in.

"You married a widower?" I said.

She nodded. I was too stunned to speak. I had finally met someone who could understand my feelings and concerns. I wasn't alone.

We talked for a long time. Despite the two decades between us, she related to every concern and worry I felt. She shared her own story about meeting and marrying a widower after her marriage ended in divorce. She told me that the key to making things work was to focus on the present and the future instead of the past.

Her words struck a chord. Most days, our marriage felt like mine and Abel's, but occasionally, reminders of his past life popped up at unexpected times and places. One evening, I was looking for a new book to read and grabbed one of Abel's books from the bookshelf. As I thumbed through the pages, I noticed underlined passages and Krista's loopy cursive handwriting in the margins. I realized this book had belonged to Krista. Several times during the first year of our marriage—and once while making love—Abel called me Krista. Once or twice when sharing a story from the past, he misremembered whether it was Krista or I who'd been with him. Another time, he had to retrieve something from one of the boxes that contained what remained of his and Krista's life together, and tears streamed down his face as he sorted through the contents. There were also moments when Abel clenched his jaw or retreated to another room, and I sensed he was angry at Krista. I rarely knew what triggered such strong emotions, but I gave him the time and space to work through them.

Though these moments were few, I wondered if it was selfish for wanting a marriage that felt like ours. After all, Krista might be part of our marriage in the next life. Perhaps this was something that wouldn't have bothered me if I was older with a past marriage of my own, but that first year together, I craved moments that only Abel and I shared.

The more I thought about it, the more I realized Krista would always play a small role. I fell in love with a man that was shaped by the loss of his late wife and daughter. Those two tragedies had molded Abel into the man I wanted to spend the eternities with. Without those experiences I doubted we could have formed the emotional and spiritual bond that was needed for us to fall in love and join our lives together. No matter where we lived or how long we were married, his past life would always be a part of him.

If my thoughts and Abel's occasional missteps had been the extent of the issues, I probably could have made peace with the unique aspects of our marriage. The most trying moments came from Abel's friends and family.

The first incident happened a few weeks after our wedding when we stopped by to visit with Abel's family. As we walked into his parents' living room, my eyes landed on a large photo of Krista, and a smaller one of Hope, which was prominently displayed in the living room. The photos had been there since my first visit. I searched for a photo of Abel and me, but I didn't see one. I figured that our marriage was recent and they hadn't gotten around to putting one up.

However, for the first two or three years of our marriage, whenever we stopped by, the photos of Krista and Hope remained while one of Abel and I never graced the room. I tried not to take it personally, but the omission stung, especially when photos of Abel's other married siblings could be found. While I didn't expect anyone to forget Krista or even take down her photo, not having one of me and Abel made it seem like our marriage wasn't important. It reached a point where I dreaded going inside their home whenever we visited.

One cold November evening, I checked the mail after coming home from work. Reaching into the mailbox, it surprised me to find several red and blue envelopes addressed to Abel. These were square envelopes that contained cards, and I didn't understand why anyone would send Abel something when it wasn't his birthday. Then the penny dropped. Krista's date of death was two days away. I read the names and return addresses. They were all from friends and family who had attended our wedding or reception. I walked into our house with my head down and tears running down my cheeks. I set the cards on the table so Abel would see them when he got home.

Abel arrived home a few minutes later. He took one look at me and asked, "What's wrong?"

"The mail," I said, motioning to the table.

Abel picked up the envelopes and shuffled through them. "Oh," he said. He didn't have to ask what the cards were for. He knew. He opened them one at a time, read them, and put them in the trash. Then he headed to our bedroom to change into more comfortable clothing.

"I got some emails today about it too," he said from the bedroom.

I sat on our bed while he changed. "Why are they sending cards and emails?" I said, trying to keep the frustration in my voice to a minimum.

"They're probably still grieving," he replied.

"But they know you're married. Why send them?"

Abel pulled on a pair of jeans. "I don't know. Maybe they think I'm still grieving too."

I realized that we had spent little time with those who had sent cards, and they probably didn't know where Abel was on his grief journey or how happy we were together. That did little to lessen the sting. "It still hurts," I said.

"I know," Abel replied.

"Will this happen every year?"

"I hope not."

"I'm sorry I'm so upset. I feel like we're making a wonderful life and then something like this happens."

Abel sat next to me on the bed and pulled me close. "No need to apologize for your feelings. I didn't see this coming either. I don't think they thought about how it would affect our relationship or what it's like for you being married to a widower."

I wiped away a tear before it fell from my cheek.

"I love you," Abel said.

"I know you do."

"What can I do to make it better?"

"Just hold me."

"Okay," Abel said as he pulled me in tighter.

We sat in silence for several minutes. Finally, Abel said, "Want to make some new memories?"

I shrugged. "What did you have in mind?"

"There's that Chinese place you like. We could go there and see where the night takes us."

The thought of food made my stomach rumble.

"I like that idea," I said.

"Change your clothes," Abel said. "Let's have some fun."

That night we stayed out late and had a great time. By the time we got into bed, I felt better. I snuggled up against Abel, grateful that he had been willing to sell his home and that we had moved to Bountiful where we could start our own life together. Though I couldn't control the thoughts or actions of others, I hoped that one day, those who were close to Abel would recognize the new life we built together.

CHAPTER THIRTY

Abel

It's time to start a family.

The thought came to my mind on a clear-blue-sky summer evening as I filled my car with gas. I was leaning against the door staring at the foothills of Bountiful in the general direction of our mother-in-law apartment. It was Friday, and one day short of our four-month anniversary and I was thinking about if I should get Julianna a small gift to mark the occasion. Having children hadn't been anywhere near the top of my mind.

The thought of starting a family filled me with excitement and dread. Being a father was something I had always looked forward to, but losing Hope had been the most devastating moment of my life. Though I had made a cautious peace with Krista's suicide, I had done little work with grieving Hope. Eighteen months after taking her off life support, I still couldn't think of her for more than a few seconds without tears welling up in my eyes.

Having kids meant the possibility of losing another child. What if he or she was stillborn? What if the baby had a disease or genetic defect that would shorten her or his life? What if something happened to Julianna? The last thought stopped me cold. Rationally, I knew the odds of losing Julianna or the baby were very small, but there was always a chance that something could go wrong.

The clunk of the gas nozzle shutting off snapped me out of my thoughts. I topped off the tank, headed home, and pushed the thought of having children to the back of my mind. As I turned down the tree-lined street that led to our apartment, the words came again as if there was a voice directly in my mind. *It's time to start a family.*

I parked in the driveway. Instead of getting out of the car, I rolled down the window to let in some fresh air while I contemplated what to do next. It was strangely quiet in the neighborhood, with only the tick-tick-tick of the cooling engine. We had discussed when and how many children we wanted before getting married. Though we didn't agree on the exact number, Julianna had agreed to wait a year before trying for kids even though she had wanted to start much sooner. I wanted children, but I didn't want a "replacement" child. I thought putting more time between Hope's death and the birth of a new one would lessen some of the sting and allow me to enjoy the experience. Julianna had gone on birth control soon after our engagement. We hadn't discussed the topic since. How would Julianna feel about starting a family sooner than planned?

We were still in the honeymoon stage, and our marriage was just about perfect. We were both training to run a marathon at the end of July, and if things went well, another one in October. We had carved out a new life for ourselves in Bountiful. Each morning, we went on long runs before work. Our evenings had fallen into familiar patterns of running errands, making dinner together, reading ourselves to sleep, and working through the occasional bump that came with merging two lives together. Our life was intimate, quiet, and drama-free. I loved what we had and didn't want to disrupt it.

When I finally headed into the apartment, I debated when to broach the subject of starting a family. Should I walk in the door and tell Julianna we needed to talk, or wait and think about it more?

Julianna sat at the kitchen table flipping through a recipe book. She had changed from her work clothes into jeans and a white form-fitting T-shirt that accentuated her figure perfectly. It was almost enough to make me want to bring up starting a family right then.

She smiled when she saw me.

"Hungry?" she said.

"Starving," I replied.

"Go change, and let's make dinner."

"It's Friday. Did you want to go out?"

"I thought we could wait until after our run tomorrow. Besides, there's a chicken parmesan recipe I want to try."

I changed into shorts and a T-shirt and returned to help with the meal. As we breaded the chicken and mixed the sauce, I considered telling her about my impression, but ultimately decided against it. Our life was just about perfect. If we didn't have the conversation, maybe the feeling would go away.

It didn't.

The next morning, the impression returned to my mind as we ran past the Bountiful Temple, and later that evening as Julianna's head rested on my shoulder after making love. Every day for the next week, thoughts about starting a family bubbled to the top of my thoughts. Each time, I pushed them to the side. No matter how often I did that, the gentle prompting kept returning. Finally, it reached a point where I couldn't hold it in any longer. At the very least, I had to ask Julianna what she thought about starting a family early.

I picked the wrong time to do it.

It was a Saturday morning—eight days after the initial prompting—and the same day we were leaving for a trip to Denver with my family to visit my grandparents and show Julianna around the city. We were packing some food for the seven-hour drive and waiting for my family so we could caravan to the Mile High City together. As we made sandwiches, the thoughts about having children weighed heavily on my mind. I positioned myself behind Julianna, put my arms around her, and kissed her on the back of the neck.

Julianna stopped working and leaned into me. I caught a whiff of her perfume and kissed her again. I leaned down and whispered in her ear, "What do you think about starting a family?"

Julianna's body stiffened.

She turned and said, "Are you serious?"

"Well, not this exact moment," I said. "My mom and dad will be here any minute."

Julianna rolled her eyes. "Is this a joke?"

"No joke. I thought we could try after running the marathon at the end of the month."

Julianna opened her mouth to reply, but a knock on our door interrupted our conversation. Through the door, I could hear the excited voices of some of my younger brothers and sisters. My family had arrived.

I gave Julianna a quick peck on the mouth.

"We'll talk more on the drive," I said, heading to the door.

The opportunity didn't present itself. My seventeen-year-old brother and fourteen-year-old sister asked if they could ride with us, and this wasn't a conversation to have in front of an audience.

Julianna showed her displeasure when an hour into our trip, I reached over to hold her hand. Instead of taking mine, she folded her arms and gave me a curt smile that spoke volumes. I knew her well enough to know she wasn't angry. Rather, she was frustrated that it would be hours before we could discuss the topic.

We finally got a moment alone when we stopped for gas and a bathroom break in Grand Junction, Colorado. As I filled the car, Julianna walked out from the gas station, and we found ourselves alone.

"Driving to Denver isn't fun when I can't hold your hand," I teased.

"You know what else isn't fun? Dropping the starting-a-family bomb right before we leave," she replied.

"My timing could have been better," I admitted. "Will you forgive me enough that I can hold your hand?"

"Are you serious about starting now?"

I nodded.

"I thought we were waiting a year. What changed your mind?"

"I feel like it's time," I said.

Before Julianna could respond, my sister returned from her bathroom break, effectively ending the conversation.

"We'll talk tonight," I said.

As I pulled onto I-70, I reached out for Julianna's hand. She pulled it away.

"I love you," I mouthed.

"I love you too," she mouthed back, then slid her hand into mine, interlocking our fingers.

I squeezed her hand.

She squeezed it back.

We drove the rest of the way to Denver holding hands.

•••

We didn't discuss our family plans again until cooling down from our run the next morning, sitting on the front lawn of my grandmother's house in Lakewood, letting the heat of the morning sun dry our sweat. It was still early and everyone else was sleeping or inside eating breakfast, so we had the yard to ourselves.

"You sure you're ready to do this?" Julianna asked. "You wanted to wait a year and we're not even to our five-month anniversary."

"I know."

Julianna wiped her brow with her shirt, lifting it high enough that I could see her flat, toned stomach. Did she even know how small acts like that turned me on?

"What changed your mind?" she said.

"I've had several strong feelings that now's the time to start."

"What kind of feelings?"

I told her about the impressions.

"You seem hesitant," I said when the quiet became uncomfortable. "I thought you'd be more excited."

"I'm thrilled," Julianna said. "I'm just surprised. Mentally, I had prepared myself to wait. I'm trying to adjust and figure out how this will impact our plans for the next few months."

The front door of the house across the street opened, and a woman wearing pink running shorts and a white tank top got in her car.

Julianna stretched her legs out on the grass. "If we're going to do this, I need to know that you're committed. I don't want you to change your mind after we've started."

"I won't change my mind," I said.

"Are you sure? Because I'm not getting off birth control unless you're mentally and emotionally ready for a pregnancy."

Her words gave me pause. Was I really ready? There were no guarantees about what would happen once Julianna conceived. Was I willing to risk the possibility, no matter how small, of more grief and sorrow that would accompany the loss of Julianna or another child? I never wanted to experience loss like that again, but couldn't let things outside of my control dictate my behavior. I commuted to work even though I might get in a fatal car accident. I ran every morning despite the risk of twisting an ankle or being hit by a car. I hadn't let Krista's death stop me from opening my heart to Julianna. If I could overcome my fears and marry Julianna, why should I let similar concerns and worries prevent me from having children?

"I'm ready to do this," I said "but you need to understand that it might be a bumpy ride."

"What does that mean?"

"My only experience with starting a family didn't end well. I can't promise you I'm going to react perfectly if problems arise with you or the baby."

"I'm not Krista."

"I know."

"I'd never hurt myself or our children."

"That's not what I'm saying."

"What are you saying, Abel?"

"When you're pregnant, I'll probably be fine most of the time, but there may be moments when something triggers me or I'm overcome with anxiety or worry. I'll do my best to push through them, but I just want to set realistic expectations."

"If you need more time to prepare yourself, I'll wait," Julianna said.

"I don't know if more time is going to make that much of a difference," I said. "Besides, I can't let fear dictate my decisions. Let's say you get pregnant, and the baby is stillborn or has a genetic defect that makes it so he or she doesn't live long after birth. All of that is beyond my control. We could have died in some horrible car accident on the way here, but we still made the trip. If I ignore these promptings, then I'm giving in to fear. I can't do that. Even though I'm scared to death about taking this step, I have faith and hope that things will work out."

A car drove slowly down the street and we sat in silence for what seemed like a long minute. Julianna reached over and touched my arm.

"If you're ready, I'm ready," she said.

"Are you sure?" I read her face for worry or concern, but there was only excitement and anticipation.

"I'm looking forward to it," she said. "Let's start right after the marathon."

"You're sure?"

"Positive. Besides, making babies is fun."

I smiled. "Yes, making babies is very, very fun."

I lay on my back and felt the soft press of the long grass and stared at the cloudless Colorado sky. This was a life-changing decision. I hoped and prayed for a happy ending.

CHAPTER THIRTY-ONE

Julianna

I pulled my shirt up to just below my breasts and stared at my stomach in the bathroom mirror. For the last two months, we'd been trying to conceive, and today was the first time I thought our efforts might have proved successful. My period was late—sort of. I was spotting. That was normal when training for marathons, but it had yet to turn into a full period. I had never spotted so long and wondered if I was pregnant. I turned sideways, hoping for a better view. It was too early to tell just by looking, but perhaps a pea-sized bulge would confirm my suspicions. I pushed against my uterus to see if it felt firmer than usual. It didn't. I certainly didn't *feel* pregnant, if there was such a thing. There was no morning sickness or nausea, no headache, and my breasts didn't feel tender. I felt tired, which I had read was one indicator of pregnancy, but Abel and I had run twelve miles that morning and over fifty miles in total that week. Being tired after that much mileage was typical.

Should I say something to Abel about my suspicions? Last month, Abel had seemed disappointed when my period arrived. I had been too, but the disappointment was fleeting and as soon as possible, we tried again. I knew some couples went for years without success, and I worried we'd find ourselves in the same situation. Perhaps one of the reasons Abel had felt prompted to start now was because conceiving would take a long time.

I wanted to surprise Abel with the news. I imagined making a cake with pink or blue frosting and having it for dessert one night and seeing how long it would take for him to gauge the significance. Then again, I thought being pregnant was something you knew or you didn't. I wasn't expecting a maybe. I tucked in my shirt and touched up my hair so Abel wouldn't wonder if something was up when I left the bathroom.

Abel was lying on the couch reading a book. He glanced up as I entered our tiny living room.

"Everything okay?" he said.

"Yep."

"Are you sure? Because your face tells a different story."

Heat rose to my cheeks. I wanted to hide my emotions better, but I loved that Abel could read me so well. It was one of the many things I loved about being married. He moved to a sitting position and patted the cushion next to him. I sat down and rested my head on his shoulder.

"I think I might be pregnant," I said.

Abel dog-eared a corner of the page and set the book on his lap. "What do you mean, 'might'?"

"I'm spotting."

Silence filled the room, but I didn't bother looking at Abel. I knew he was mentally calculating when my period should arrive. I knew him well too.

"We ran a lot of miles this week," he said.

"Not as much as usual."

"We ran twelve miles this morning."

"I know."

"Do you feel different?"

"What do you mean?"

"Any morning sickness? Tender boobs?"

"No. Nothing."

More silence. Finally, Abel said, "Why don't we go to the store and buy a pregnancy test? That way we can know for sure."

Why hadn't I thought of that?

"Right now?"

"Do you want to know or not?"

I wanted to know.

Despite the lateness of the hour, we drove to the nearest store and bought a box with two tests. I was so lost in thought about whether I was pregnant and how that would change our life that I missed the knowing look the cashier gave us as we bought it—something Abel laughed about on the drive home. Fifteen minutes later, I was back in the bathroom. We had agreed that I could see the results before sharing them. I stood over the sink and held the test in my hand, waiting to see if the second line appeared.

On the other side of the door, I heard Abel pacing. The kitchen was small enough that Abel could only take three steps before turning around. I wondered how he would react to either result. Would he be excited? Disappointed? Worried?

Finally, I broke out of my thoughts and looked at the test.

Two lines.

I was pregnant.

A thrill of excitement rushed through me. I—we—were going to have a baby.

I opened the bathroom door and threw my arms around Abel and exclaimed, "I'm pregnant!"

"Are you sure?"

I showed Abel the test. He squeezed me back and said, "I'm so happy."

For the next few weeks, we basked in the excitement. Then we took a vacation to Seattle, and everything changed.

•••

I had looked forward to our trip to Seattle for months. There were many reasons why, but the biggest was the opportunity it gave the two of us to make new memories. Abel had never been to Seattle, and I wanted to show him the city and the surrounding area. This would be our first trip as a couple that had no connection to his past life. At two months pregnant, it was the perfect time to go.

The first day, we pushed through the twelve-hour drive and spent the next two days touring Seattle. We took rides on the ferries, visited the Space Needle, the waterfront, and various museums. We visited new restaurants and tried their food. We spent a day in Tacoma, where I showed him the house and neighborhood where I grew up, followed by a tour of the University of Puget Sound. The days were fun-filled and memorable, and each night, we went to bed exhausted.

On the fourth morning, I woke up with an upset stomach and headache. I chalked this up to pushing myself too hard over the last three days. I told Abel I didn't feel well, and he suggested a rest day. I decided to continue with our plans, but at a slower pace. However, by the time lunch rolled around, I felt worse. I had cramps, chills, and was so nauseated, I couldn't eat. At that point, Abel called off the rest of our activities, and we headed back to the hotel to rest, thinking that a nap and staying off our feet would help.

We spent the afternoon in bed watching a movie. Really, Abel watched, while I closed my eyes. The headache and queasy feeling didn't subside and I couldn't sleep. After a few hours of tossing and turning, I used the bathroom and noticed blood. I was spotting. My first thought was about the baby. What if there was a complication with the pregnancy?

My mind raced. Had I overexerted myself on the trip? Should I have cut back on my running? What if I had done something that hurt the baby? I left the bathroom in tears.

"What's wrong?" Abel said.

"I think I'm having a miscarriage," I said.

Abel sat up straight. "Are you sure?"

"I don't know. I've never been pregnant before."

Abel went to work. Within minutes, we were out the door, and he was on the phone with my insurance provider, explaining the situation and asking for directions to the closest hospital. Thankfully, there was one less than ten minutes away, and Abel drove there as quickly as possible. After being admitted, we found ourselves in a curtained room waiting for what seemed like an hour for a doctor to show up. While we waited, I silently prayed that we would not lose the baby and that the doctor could figure out what was wrong. I hoped I hadn't done something that might have caused this to happen.

Abel squeezed my hand, bringing me out of my thoughts. All things considered, he was handling this situation well. I appreciated his calm demeanor, even though I could tell by his furrowed brow and the way he kept adjusting his baseball cap that he was worried.

"It will be okay," he said.

"What if I lose the baby?"

"She'll be fine."

"What if the baby doesn't make it?"

"Let's not focus on that. The fact that the doctor isn't rushing in here makes me think they're not too worried."

Beyond the curtain, I could hear the beeps of medical machinery and the distant chatter of nurses.

"Do you think our baby's a girl?" I asked.

Abel gave me a quizzical look. "I have no idea."

"A moment ago, you said 'she'."

"I did?"

"You did."

"Okay, I guess I did."

"Do you want a girl?"

"I just want a healthy baby and a healthy wife."

"I hope all the walking didn't cause this."

"It didn't. I know you love our baby and would never hurt her."

I squeezed Abel's hand. "You said 'her'."

Abel smiled and said, "I guess I did."

The doctor pulled back the curtain and walked in. He checked my vitals and asked a series of questions. Then he said, "Sounds like a urinary tract infection."

"Are you sure?" My symptoms seemed too serious for something so simple.

The doctor nodded. "I'll write a prescription that will clear it up."

A wave of relief swept over me. Abel leaned back in his seat and let out a breath.

"The baby's healthy?" I asked the doctor.

"Your baby's fine. Take the prescription and stay off your feet for a couple of days. Oh, and drink lots of cranberry juice."

We left the hospital late that night tired, but relieved. We found a twenty-four-hour pharmacy and filled the prescription. The next morning, we cut our trip short and headed home. We did the long drive in one day and spent the rest of our vacation holed up in our apartment reading, sleeping, and watching movies. When Monday morning rolled around, I felt like myself.

Driving to work, I thought about the trip. We had created unique memories although some I wasn't expecting. But the memories themselves didn't matter. Abel had handled a stressful situation and a triggering event perfectly. While he could have let his loss or emotions take over, he stood strong. Never again would I worry about him not being emotionally ready to start a family or a new chapter of his life. The baby was healthy. In seven months, Abel and I would be parents. I couldn't wait for him or her to arrive.

CHAPTER THIRTY-TWO

Abel

It wasn't until the New Year that I noticed a small bulge in Julianna's belly as she changed into pajamas one night before bed.

"I can see the baby," I said.

Julianna pulled up her shirt several inches. "You finally noticed the bump?"

"How long has it been there?"

"A couple weeks."

"Why didn't you say anything?"

"I wanted to see if you would notice."

We got into bed, and I rested my hand on the bump. I knew it was too soon to feel any movement, but something tangible made the experience more real. Until this moment, Julianna's pregnancy was like a pleasant dream. Now that I could feel her uterus growing, reality set in. Potential complications cascaded through my mind. Hypertension. Infections. Preeclampsia. Mental health issues. I didn't verbalize my concerns or want to burden Julianna with my worries. Instead, I prayed that the pregnancy would be uneventful.

To quiet my fears, I attended every prenatal visit with Julianna—something I hadn't done with Krista. Because Krista's doctor was in Ogden, attending her appointments wasn't possible without taking an entire morning or afternoon off work, and I was hoping to save as much time as possible for when the baby came. Besides, finances had been tight, and we needed to earn and save every dollar. Not attending Krista's prenatal exams was one of my remaining regrets. If I had been there, would I have picked up on something? Did the doctor express concerns that were never passed on? There was no way to know. All I could do was not make that same mistake twice. If there were any concerns about the baby, Julianna, or the pregnancy, I wanted to know about it.

However, each prenatal exam was uneventful. The doctor and physician assistants appeared happy with Julianna's health and the baby's development. As the pregnancy progressed, it surprised the doctor that Julianna was still running, but his only advice was not to overextend herself. Though I still worried about Julianna and the baby, being part of these visits kept my concerns at a manageable level.

Or so I thought.

One afternoon when we stopped by Julianna's family home for a visit, I was taking off my shoes and Julianna headed to the family room to chat with four of her sisters. It had been several weeks since our last visit, and I expected them to ooh and ah over Julianna's growing belly. Instead, their first questions were about me.

"How's Abel holding up?" one of them asked.

"He's doing good," Julianna replied.

"Is he freaking out yet?" another sister asked.

"No," Julianna said.

A third asked, "Is he still going with you to the doctor?"

"He's there for every visit."

My heart sank at the words. This was Julianna's first pregnancy, and they should have focused their attention on her. I didn't blame my sisters-in-law for asking those questions, but it made me evaluate how well I was doing. Were there unconscious tells that made them worry?

On the drive home, I brought up the subject.

"How do you think I'm handling your pregnancy?"

Julianna took a moment to think it over. "You're doing better than I expected," she said. She took my hand in hers and asked, "How are you really doing?"

I let the question hang in the air while deciding the best way to answer it.

"I still worry that something will happen to you or the baby," I finally admitted.

"Like what?"

I shrugged. "Lots of things. Miscarriage. Fatal genetic defects. A stillbirth. Some rare disease."

"Are you worried that I'll hurt myself or the baby?"

"No. That's at the bottom of the list."

"But it's something you think about."

"It has crossed my mind."

Julianna let go of my hand. "Have I done or said anything that makes you think I would harm myself or our child?"

"No, of course not."

"Then why think it?"

"Based on my experience, how could I not?"

A contemplative silence permeated the car as we both worked through what to say next.

"I'm not comparing you," I finally said. "I'm being extra vigilant."

Julianna sighed. "I don't feel compared. I just wish the pregnancy could be something that didn't trigger thoughts of the past."

"It will be different when baby number two comes," I said. "This first experience is something we need to work through together."

"I know," she said. "Still . . ."

Her voice trailed off. I held out my hand. Julianna took it, sliding her fingers between mine.

"When the baby's born, that will be a first for both of us, and before you say anything about Hope, remember that I never witnessed her birth."

"That's right," Julianna said. "I forgot about that."

"The birth of our child is something I want to see more than anything," I said.

Julianna squeezed my hand. "Thanks," she said. "It's something I want you to be at my side and experience together."

• • •

It turned out that I didn't have to wait for the baby to come to feel like I was plowing new ground. That happened when we found out the baby's gender. I was nervous and excited as the ultrasound technician smoothed warm gel on Julianna's abdomen and began examining the baby. My top concern was finding a genetic defect or deformity that would cause a premature death or stillbirth. I knew the odds were small, but couldn't shoulder the death of another child. The exam went quickly, and as the technician measured the length of bones, heart, and other organs, I relaxed. We had a strong, healthy baby.

"Do you want to know the baby's gender?" the technician asked.

"Yes!" we both exclaimed at the same time.

Julianna and I looked at each other and laughed. We turned our attention to the screen as the technician repositioned the transducer.

I hoped the baby was a girl. At the time, I couldn't explain those feelings but now, with nearly two decades of hindsight, I thought having a girl would ease the pain and sting of losing Hope. It wasn't rational to think that the birth of one baby would erase the loss of another, but that's where my emotions drifted.

"Any guesses?" the technician asked.

"Girl!" I said.

Julianna said nothing. Her attention was focused on the screen.

The technician positioned the transducer, and the screen showed the baby's bottom. The penis was hard to miss.

"It's a boy," the technician said.

A boy. We were having a boy.

Julianna squeezed my hand as if to ask if I was all right.

"Wow," I said. "A boy."

"You seem surprised."

"I am," I said. "I thought it was going to be a girl."

"Are you okay with a boy?"

"I'm fine with a boy. I'm just glad he's healthy."

On the drive home, we discussed boy names. We didn't agree on any of them, but for me, knowing it was a boy made the pregnancy fresh, new, and exciting.

•••

The firsts continued piling up. Julianna's friends and family held a baby shower, and suddenly baby clothes, a car seat, bottles, and diapers filled our apartment. We splurged and bought a wooden crib that Julianna said could be used for our kids and any grandkids that would eventually come. Setting up the crib was exciting and made the baby's arrival feel imminent and real.

Realizing our current apartment wasn't large enough for the three of us, we moved to a bigger place that was closer to my work and Julianna's family. Prenatal exams became more frequent, but were uneventful. According to the doctor, Julianna and the baby were both strong and healthy. Fantasies of Julianna waking me up at two in the morning to drive to the hospital replaced thoughts and worries about stillbirths or other complications.

One night about a month before the baby's birth, Julianna was sleeping and I rested my arm around her belly, hoping to feel the baby move. I did the math and realized Julianna had carried this baby longer than Krista had carried Hope. I said a silent prayer of gratitude that we had made it this far without incident.

When it was time for the baby to come, instead of my hoped-for middle-of-the-night trip to the hospital, Julianna had a scheduled induction date. That morning, we got up, showered, double-checked that we had packed everything, and drove to the hospital. I followed the speed limit and came to complete stops. Even though the drive was uneventful, I was ecstatic. Before the end of the day, I was going to be a father again.

The hospital admitted us, the doctor induced labor, and the waiting game began. We had brought some movies and a portable DVD player to help pass the time, but I couldn't concentrate on the screen. Instead, I thought about the birth of our son and how this one event was going to change my life forever. This moment was the payoff for the leap of faith I had taken almost a year earlier. I closed my eyes and said a silent prayer that both Julianna and the baby would be healthy and the delivery would be without incident.

Eventually Julianna's labor became more intense, and I turned off the movie. We held hands while Julianna worked through one contraction after another. At some point, a nurse checked on Julianna's progress and announced the baby was coming soon. She paged a doctor, and soon the room filled with nurses and others to assist in the delivery. Everyone but me seemed to know what to do, so I held Julianna's hand and watched as she pushed through a contraction. Minutes later, the crown of the baby's head was visible. Two more pushes, and his head fully emerged.

His head was facing toward me. His eyes fluttered open, and before a last push sent him into the hands of the doctor, he looked right at me. A warm, peaceful feeling filled my body, and all the worries and concerns about his and Julianna's health vanished.

Nurses checked the baby's vitals before wrapping him in a blanket and handing him to Julianna. I sat next to the bed and watched Julianna talk to the baby and try to get him to nurse. He didn't want to eat, so Julianna asked if I wanted to hold him.

I took the baby and held him in my arms. He blinked, yawned, and rubbed his hand against his face. He was healthy. He was alive. My mind flashed back to Hope and how different that experience had been. In the nine days of her life, she had done none of those things on her own. I held the baby close and let the tears run down my cheeks.

"What's wrong?" Julianna asked.

"Nothing. I'm happy to have a healthy wife and baby," I said.

It was mostly true. Some tears were for the daughter I never got the chance to raise, but most were tears of joy—for the second chance to be a father and starting a family with Julianna.

CHAPTER THIRTY-THREE

Julianna

Having a baby changed everything. We named him Aidan and he upended my daily routines and sleeping patterns. Our apartment was never as clean as I wanted. I could no longer just jump in the car to run errands, go to church, or visit family. Trips, no matter how small, needed to be planned around his feeding schedules and naps. I exercised and ran when Abel was home. Date nights evolved from dinners out or time spent at a sporting event to rented movies that we would both usually sleep through. It was quite an adjustment for someone who thrived on routine and schedules, but with Abel's help, I made it work.

Aidan also refocused all of my thoughts and energy on our family. I didn't have the time to worry about whether Abel had done something similar with Krista or if she was going to be part of my marriage in the next life. I was too busy with Aidan and learning to be a mom to care about much else.

What surprised me the most was the effect his arrival had on Abel's family and friends. Overnight emails, cards, and reminders about Krista stopped. Many who had contacted Abel on the second anniversary of Krista's death now sent congratulatory cards and emails on our new arrival. The first time we visited Abel's family with Aidan, his mom took countless photos of the three of us.

My heart expanded and grew in ways I never thought possible. I was always told the human heart has a great capacity for love, but it took having Aidan to show me how big it can grow. Though I was hesitant to make a direct comparison to loving multiple children with multiple spouses, it helped me understand how Abel could love me and still hold a special place in his heart for Krista.

Six months after Aidan's birth, we bought our first home. That purchase kept both of us busy painting the walls, finishing the basement, and doing other tasks that made the house feel like ours. Eighteen months after Aidan's birth a second child, Steven, arrived. Life became even busier. We bought a double-wide running stroller so we could run together as a family. Between work, raising children, training for marathons, and everything it took to keep our home running, I went to bed every night exhausted. But it was a good tired, and I wouldn't have traded my marriage and our family for anything.

And mostly the past stayed in its proper place, but now and then, reminders popped up at unexpected times.

Two months before Steven's birth, I went to the mailbox and found a card addressed to Abel and I. I didn't recognize the name on the return address. Inside was a wedding invitation. I recognized the groom as someone from Krista's family that I had met once, but I couldn't place the relationship.

"He's Krista's cousin," Abel said later that evening when he read the invitation. "He lived with Loretta for a time when Krista and I were married. Do you want to go?"

I was unsure. Since our marriage, contact with Krista's family had been minimal. I was nervous about attending. Were they still grieving? How would they react to seeing Abel and I together? I was about as far along in my pregnancy as Krista had been when she died. Would my protruding belly cause flashbacks?

As if sensing my concerns, Abel said, "You don't have to come. I can go alone."

"I should go," I said. "I can't let unfounded worries stop me from living my life."

"I'm glad you'll be there," Abel said. "I'd prefer you were at my side."

"Do you think there will be any issues with her family seeing the two of us together?"

Abel shrugged. "Probably not. I don't think they would have invited us if there were major concerns."

My worries turned out to be unfounded. The wedding and lunch were uneventful. Everyone seemed glad to see us, and all of the attention was on the bride and groom.

After the ceremony, as Abel caught up with Scott and other members of Krista's extended family, I found myself at a table with Loretta. I was nervous and unsure what to say. Before our marriage, I'd only had some brief interactions with her. The last time I saw her was at our wedding reception.

"It's nice to see you and Abel again," Loretta said, scooting her chair closer to mine. "Where are you living now?"

"Eagle Mountain. It's a new city in northern Utah County."

"How's the pregnancy? This is number two, right?"

"Yes, it's our second."

"Boy? Girl?"

"A boy."

"How exciting! Your first child was a boy, right?"

"Yes," I said. It felt good that she knew so much about our family.

"Do you have a name picked out?"

"We've narrowed it down to two names, but haven't decided yet. We want to wait until the baby's born."

As the conversation continued, I relaxed. The two of us continued talking about babies and life. There was no mention of Krista. I didn't know where Loretta was in the grieving process, but it meant the world to me that we could have a normal conversation.

On the drive home, Abel said, "I saw you and Loretta talking. How did that go?"

"It was great. This was the first time I've really talked to her."

"How is she doing?"

"She seemed happy and at peace."

"I'm glad," Abel said. "Scott was the same way. Talking to him felt like a conversation we would have had before Krista died."

For the first time since marrying Abel, I felt like others who had strong ties to Krista were moving forward with their lives. It gave me hope that we could now attend events without the past hanging over the invitations.

•••

A few months after the wedding, Loretta unexpectedly passed away. This time, there wasn't any discussion if I would attend. We both were going. I wondered how Abel would handle the barrage of memories the funeral might trigger, but that was out of my control. I went to support Abel and pay my respects to Loretta.

I recognized many faces at the funeral from the wedding. The service was a happy affair and celebrated Loretta's life and accomplishments more than mourning her loss. Abel had previously mentioned that she had spent most of her golden years raising Krista and Scott, but it wasn't until I heard stories about her that I began to understand just how much time she had devoted to raising two of her grandchildren. I admired that she had voluntarily spent two decades of her life being their mother so they could have a better future.

Abel handled things well. There were some tears and stories about Krista and Loretta, but that was expected. The only thing that stood out was a comment Abel made on the drive home. He noted how different funerals are when the person had lived a long, full life instead of one that was cut short. I knew he was thinking about Krista's funeral and comparing it with Loretta's. I didn't know how to respond, so I said nothing. Abel seemed a little down the rest of the day, but by the next morning, he was back to normal.

Despite the progress, reminders of Abel's past life popped up at unexpected times. The one that stands out the most happened soon after Loretta's funeral. I went out to get the mail and found a package from Abel's mom addressed to both of us. Upon opening it, I found two old news articles about Krista's suicide, an obituary clipping of a young man whose name I didn't recognize, and a copy of a speech that was given at the person's funeral. There was no letter or note that explained the reason for sending it.

I wish I had responded to this surprise package better by, say, putting it to the side and asking Abel about it when he came home. Instead, I scanned the articles, read the obituary, and the talk. I had seen the two articles about Krista's death previously as Abel had kept copies in his journal. The obituary was of a young man in his early thirties named Matthew. I didn't recognize the name or his photo. A cause of death wasn't mentioned but for some reason I knew Matthew had killed himself. Then I read the talk and my suspicions were confirmed.

The talk was given at Matthew's funeral by his stake president. Stake presidents are lay leaders of geographic regions called a stake, which is similar to a Catholic diocese. The stake president had addressed Matthew's suicide and directed his words to Matthew's family and friends. He spoke about the pain and anguish they were feeling then told them not to despair when it came to the state of Matthew's soul. God would administer fair judgement and would take into account Matthew's state of mind, circumstances, and degree of accountability. He wrapped up his speech by talking about the miracle of eternal families and how those in attendance would see their son, brother, and friend again in the next life.

The stake president's speech echoed a common refrain in Latter-day Saint teachings. I assumed Abel's mom had mailed it because she thought it would give Abel peace and comfort, but including the articles about Krista made me feel like she was sending a not-so-subtle reminder that he had another wife waiting for him. I didn't know how Abel would react, but reading those words rekindled emotions and reminders about my unknown status in the next life. It seemed when the subject of suicide or eternal families came up, everyone always thought about Krista's salvation first and foremost. Abel's well-being or my struggles of possibly being a second wife in heaven were always an afterthought. Even though I loved that Abel and I were sealed in an eternal bond, I loathed the possibility of sharing Abel with Krista or anyone else in the next life.

Tears welled up in my eyes. I tossed the speech on the kitchen table, put Aidan in his car seat, and drove to my parents' house. Maybe it was the stress of the day trying to get work done and taking care of Aidan combined with pregnancy hormones. Perhaps it was because for the last year, I had felt that our marriage was finally feeling like ours, and this unexpected delivery had arrived at exactly the wrong time. Whatever the reason, I couldn't stay in the same house with that package.

I had mostly calmed down when I reached my parents' home forty-five minutes later, but by the concerned look on my mom's face when she answered the door, I wasn't doing a good job of hiding my feelings.

"What's wrong?" she asked.

For the second time that day, I broke down in tears. When I had recovered enough to tell her what was going on, she hugged me.

"I don't have the words to help you," she said. "I wish I could make things better."

"I feel horrible for reacting this way," I said. "I knew there'd be moments like this when Abel and I got married. I didn't expect a smooth ride, but things have been wonderful since Aidan was born. It was a surprise to find that in the mail."

"I don't understand why she would send that talk," my mom said.

"The obituary would be one thing but it was the talk and news articles that really stung," I replied. "The last thing I need is reminders that Krista might be waiting for Abel... That sounds awful but all I want is normal marriage and a normal life—one free of reminders that I might be wife number two in the eternities."

"You're shouldering a burden I couldn't carry," my mom said giving me an extra squeeze. "My heart breaks when I see your anguish and what you're going through."

"I wish more people were understood what it's like to be sealed to a widower," I said. "Spiritual polygamy isn't a topic we discuss at church or anywhere else. You'd think there'd be talks or other church resources that I could turn to but there's nothing. Whenever thoughts and worries about Krista and the eternities come up, I feel so alone."

We continued talking. My mom couldn't answer any of my questions or concerns but she listened and did her best to comfort me. By the time Abel called after returning from work and finding me gone, I had settled down enough to take his call.

"Where are you?" he said. Worry and concern weaved through his question.

"At my parents'."

"Why are you there?"

"Check the kitchen table."

I heard Abel's footsteps as he moved from whatever room he was in to the kitchen. There was a long silence before he spoke.

"I didn't know this was coming."

"I know. Why did your mom send it to you?"

I heard the scraping of paper over the phone.

"I knew Matthew. We went to church together as teenagers."

278

Not knowing what to say, I let the silence ride. Maybe that was a reason his mom had sent the package.

Finally, Abel spoke, "Maybe my mom wanted to let me know about Matthew's death, or perhaps she thought the stake president's words would help with unanswered questions about Krista and the eternities."

"I wish more people understood just how hard it is to be a second wife. I love that we can be together forever but I still don't know where I fit in. It stings when I think of sharing you."

Both of us went quiet. Finally, Abel asked, "Are you mad at me?"

"No."

"Are you coming home?"

"Yes."

"When?"

"Soon. I need to feed Aidan first, and my mom has invited me to eat dinner here."

"If you leave now, I'll make something delicious and have it ready by the time you get here," Abel said.

"I still need some time to think things over."

Abel reluctantly agreed. I ate dinner with my family and put Aidan to sleep before driving home. There I found Abel sitting in our bed, writing. He closed his laptop as I walked in. He looked like he was ready to fall asleep at any minute, and I realized we were usually in bed by this time. However, I was glad that Abel had waited up. I lay on top of the covers and rested my head on his shoulder.

"Are you doing better?" he asked.

"More or less back to normal," I said.

"I'm glad you're back. It's not fun spending the evening alone."

"Do you think I overreacted?"

"No, but I wish you had called me. After I got home and found you gone, I worried you had left me."

"I would never do that."

"You're the number-one woman in my heart."

"You're not the problem," I said as I slipped under the covers.

Abel pulled me close, and I rested my head on his shoulder. For a long time, we lay in silence lost in our own thoughts, our own worlds.

"What did you do for dinner?" I finally said.

"Microwaved the leftover casserole."

"Did you get a lot of writing done?"

Abel chuckled. "Nope. I was too worried about you. Besides, the silence in this house is awful. It reminded me how much I hate being alone."

"Did you read the stake president's talk?"

"I did."

"Any insights?"

Abel shook his head. "Nothing I didn't already know. It was about accepting that we won't understand everything in this life, and a just and merciful God will judge us in the next one. But the speech wasn't for me—it was for Matthew's family. I hope they found it comforting."

"How well did you know Matthew?"

"Not well. I saw him at church on Sundays. Sometimes we hung out at church activities and camps, but we went to different high schools and ran in different social circles," Abel said.

"He never struck me as depressed or suicidal, but Krista didn't come off that way either."

"If you weren't good friends, why even send it? Maybe I'd be more understanding if the two of you were close, but the news articles about Krista's death and the talk make me feel like Krista comes first. I don't expect anyone to forget about her but today it felt like I didn't matter and that our marriage isn't as important as your marriage to her."

Abel rubbed my arm. "Your number one in my heart."

"Am I?"

"Do you doubt it?"

"No," I said. "Not now. Not in this life, anyway. I just wish there was a clearer understanding of the next one."

A topic we hadn't discussed in years swirled around my head. This seemed like a good time to discuss, since I didn't know when the opportunity would come up again.

"Do you still think you and Krista will be together in heaven?"

Abel let out a long breath before answering. "I have no idea. I don't think anyone does."

"How do you want things to work out?"

"I want her to be at my side as much I want you there. The next life would be incomplete without both of you, Hope, Aidan, and the baby growing inside you."

It wasn't the answer I wanted, even if it was expected. I had come to peace with a lot of things regarding Krista, but I still wanted Abel all to myself.

"That's not what you wanted to hear," Abel said.

"It's not," I admitted. "I still wonder how her suicide will affect things."

"I'm sure it will have some effect, but I don't know how much. No one does."

I thought back to the prompting I'd had years earlier about Abel and our kids all being in the temple together. I reminded myself of the choice I had made to continue the relationship with Abel and the peace I felt from that decision. I reminded myself that I couldn't control what happened to Krista in the next life. Perhaps she'd be part of our marriage. Maybe not. All I could focus on was being a good wife, mother, daughter, sister, friend, and neighbor. I thought about my reaction to the package and felt I had failed in that regard. I vowed to do better.

I got out of bed, changed into pajamas, and brushed my teeth. When I got back to our bedroom, Abel had turned off the lights and was lying on his back. I got into bed and turned so he could spoon me. He wrapped his arms around me and kissed the top of my head. I lay there and let his warmth envelop me.

While enjoying the moment, I thought about all the blessings I received from my decision to move forward with Abel. I had a husband who loved me, a son I adored, and a second son on the way. We had a lovely home and food on the table. What more did I need to be happy? I turned over and gave Abel a long, passionate kiss. "I love you," I said and kissed him again.

The next morning, I woke up feeling Abel's body pressed against mine. I was happy that we had a life together that we could call our own.

CHAPTER THIRTY-FOUR

Abel

On Halloween night 2007, I left work early to take Aidan and Steven, ages three and two, trick-or-treating together. Going around the neighborhood was one of those dad moments I looked forward to. Last year I had carried Aidan to three or four homes, but he had been uninterested in the activity, and we'd abandoned the effort. I hoped this year would be different. Maybe with his brother in tow, we could make it around the neighborhood.

A block from home, I stopped at the corner as a procession of monsters, superheroes, and Harry Potter characters crossed the street. Even with the windows up, I heard their excited chatter and imagined Aidan and Steven having the same enthusiasm as we went from house to house. I spotted a girl with brown hair wearing a tiara and a purple princess dress. She appeared to be five or six years old. She tightly gripped her mother's hand while in the other she held the handle to a black bucket with pictures of bats, cats, and witches. There was something about her age and the brown hair that triggered thoughts about Hope.

Hope should be trick-or-treating too, I thought. I imagined her dressed as a princess accompanying the boys and I around the neighborhood. A flashback of Hope taking her last breaths in my arms quickly followed. Anger toward Krista surged through my veins as I thought about the life and experiences Hope had missed. I gripped the steering wheel tightly and cursed Krista under my breath.

The next month would mark six years since Krista had taken her own life. Moments of anger had become less frequent, but when they occurred, they still burned white hot. I wondered if the feelings of anger and betrayal would ever go away. I hated feeling this way, but the wounds Krista left were so deep and personal, maybe they'd never heal.

The car behind me honked, bringing me out of my thoughts. I eased through the intersection, holding back tears as I drove the rest of the way home. Whenever anger toward Krista overwhelmed me, I usually put some physical distance between myself and Julianna so I could work through my feelings alone either in silence or sometimes on my knees. For several minutes, I sat in the garage and waited for my anger to cool. I didn't want to come into the house upset and possibly ruin what promised to be a fun evening. When I felt calm enough to force a smile, I headed inside.

Aidan and Steven hugged my legs when I walked in the door. Aidan wore a Batman costume with a mask that kept sliding off his face. Steven was dressed up as a robot. Our daughter, Molly, not quite one, sat in her high chair and smiled at me, smears of baby food covering her mouth and cheeks. She wasn't wearing a costume.

Julianna gave me a kiss and said, "Everything okay?"

After four years of marriage, she knew when something was off.

"I'm fine," I said and gave her a peck on the lips. Before she could pursue that line of questioning, I looked at the boys, who were still hugging my legs, and said, "You ready to go trick-or-treating?"

"Yes!" Aidan said.

"Do you want some dinner first?" Julianna asked.

"Did the kids eat?" I said, though the table of orange-streaked macaroni plates and half-empty glasses of water told me the answer.

"They just finished," Julianna said.

"I'll eat later."

A knock on the door and the muffled sound of "Trick-or-treat!" interrupted our conversation. Julianna went to pass out some candy while I put coats on the boys. Two minutes later, we headed out the door. The boys carried orange plastic pumpkins to hold candy. However, instead of hurrying to the neighbor's house, they walked at a leisurely pace and appeared more interested in looking at the costumes the other kids wore.

When we arrived at the next-door neighbor's home, I explained to Aidan how to trick-or-treat. He knocked on the door, but it was so timid, I assumed the neighbor didn't hear it.

"Knock harder," I said.

Aidan rapped on the door again. A moment later, a neighbor, an older man with white hair and a beard, opened the door holding a big bowl of candy.

"Hello, Batman," the neighbor said.

Aidan's eyes went from the neighbor back to me.

"Tell him 'Trick or treat,'" I said.

Aidan stared at the neighbor, but said nothing. The neighbor chuckled and put a mini candy bar in Aidan's bucket and handed Steven a piece of candy. I thanked him, and it was off to the next house. As we walked, I explained the trick-or-treating routine to both boys again.

At the next house, Aidan knocked loud and said "Trick or treat!" but he appeared unsure what the fuss was about. Steven held up his bucket and smiled when someone dropped a piece of candy in it. This went on until we reached the end of the block. Aidan checked his bucket and gave me a bored look showing he was ready to go home.

"Do you want more candy?"

Aidan reached into his bucket and took out a mini candy bar. "Can I have this?" he said.

"Yes, but we need to go home first."

Aidan turned and started toward home. I followed, holding Steven's hand. I felt bummed that Halloween had been a fifteen-minute trip to the end of the block. But that was okay. There was always next year.

On the walk back, we passed a pack of trick-or-treaters, and I noted the two princesses in the group. That triggered another flashback of Hope, but instead of being sad or angry, I thought about how life rarely turned out the way we expected. Though I would have loved to have her trick-or-treating with Aidan and Steven, I was spending time with my boys and enjoying the moment.

"Back so soon?" Julianna said as we walked in the door.

"They wanted to eat their candy," I explained.

I helped the boys off with their coats and sat at the kitchen table and watched them open their candy. Molly sat in her high chair and smeared a piece of chocolate across her mouth. Julianna passed out some candy to a group of pirates, robots, and superheroes, then joined us at the table. As Aidan and Steven ate their candy, tears welled up in my eyes as I realized how blessed I was to have a family again. Julianna, Aidan, Steven, and Molly were the most important people in my life. I had worked hard—very hard—to build a life with them, and I wanted nothing more than to spend this one and the next with them as an eternal family.

Unexpectedly, a warm, peaceful feeling started in my chest and spread until it filled my entire body. As it expanded, the warmth purged all the anger and resentment I held toward Krista. In a matter of seconds, six years of tears, hurt, rage, and bitterness vanished. The unanswered questions surrounding her suicide no longer mattered. The grief, sorrow, and sting of Hope's death disappeared too. For years, I had wrestled with these dark feelings and despite my best efforts, I could never fully extinguish them. Yet in seconds, this feeling had reached to the farthest and deepest part of my soul and cleansed it.

The peaceful feeling was accompanied by a physical component. It felt like someone had lifted an anvil off my chest—a weight had lain there for so long that I'd grown accustomed to it. As the warmth spread, I felt physically lighter. I could breathe easier and sit up straighter now that this heavy burden was gone.

I was free.

I was free.

I was free.

Julianna glanced up as I wiped my eyes with the back of my hands. "What's wrong?" she asked, lines of worry etched on her forehead.

"Everything's fine," I said. "I was just thinking how blessed I am to have all of you in my life."

We spent the next twenty minutes eating candy and telling the boys not-so-scary stories. After we got the three kids in bed, Julianna and I sat side by side on the couch. She leaned her head on my shoulder. I took her hand and we sat in silence, relishing the moment of quiet.

"Did you still have a good time even though you came back early?" she asked.

"I did," I said and told her about Aidan getting bored and the boys' reactions to knocking on doors and neighbors putting candy in their buckets. Even though the evening hadn't turned out how I'd envisioned, it was the unexpected change of heart that made it memorable.

The sound of muffled voices approaching the house interrupted my thoughts. The doorbell rang, followed by a chorus of young voices yelling "Trick or treat!"

"Your turn," Julianna said.

"Do I have to?"

"Give them the rest of the candy and turn off the light. I'm ready for bed."

On our porch stood four girls and a boy with smiles and open bags.

One girl wore a princess costume, and for a moment, my thoughts returned to Hope. Only this time, no tears or anger accompanied the memory.

I emptied the remaining candy into their bags, giving a few more pieces to the one dressed as a princess. I turned off the porch light and locked the door. On the way to bed, I checked on my kids. They were all sound asleep.

In bed, I put my arms around Julianna and pulled her close. I kissed the back of her neck.

"I love you most times eternity," I said.

"I love you most times eternity too."

Soon, we were both asleep.

I was never angry at Krista again.

CHAPTER THIRTY-FIVE

Julianna

I hung a framed photograph of our fifth child, Brecklyn, on the wall then took a step back to admire my work. I straightened one frame then examined the collection again. Five chubby, wide-eyed faces smiled at me. Happy with the arrangement, I wondered how soon after getting home from work Abel would notice the new addition.

When Abel and I became parents, we decided to get professional photographs of our children about a month after their birth and hang them on our living room wall. Each photograph brought a feeling of delight and accomplishment. Yet, while looking at these photos, I felt strongly someone was missing.

All my children are here, I thought. *No one is missing.*

Was it time to have another child? No, that wasn't it. After taking a moment to listen, trying to understand the impression, I realized the missing child was Hope.

The delighted cries of our three oldest kids brought me out of my thoughts. As I watched Aidan, now seven, Steven, six, Molly five, and Brennan, two, run around the room playing an impromptu game of tag, I realized they knew nothing about their half-sister. They didn't even know their father had been married before. I could point to the kitchen table that we'd never replaced and a few other pieces of furniture that had come with Abel when we merged households, but there was nothing obvious that indicated he had a past life.

We had both worked hard to make our marriage feel like ours. We had succeeded, and yet, in the process, we had somehow buried Abel's past. In part, this was because we had both reached a quiet peace with Abel's former life. I no longer worried about how his marriage to Krista might affect our relationship in the next life and Abel hadn't shown any anger toward her in years. Our collective focus was on the things we could control: strengthening our marriage and caring for our children.

My stomach clenched at the thought of having an in-depth conversation with Abel about adding a photo of Hope. Two or three times since moving to our home in Eagle Mountain I suggested hanging a photograph of his daughter somewhere in our home but Abel had refused and I hadn't pushed the issue. Perhaps this time the conversation would go differently.

After getting our kids down for the night, Abel opened his laptop to write. Instead of reading a book, I lay on top of the covers next to him and watched his fingers fly across the keyboard. After a few minutes he yawned and stretched his arms. It seemed like a good time to bring it up.

"We have wonderful kids," I said.

"That we do," Abel replied, staring at the screen.

"I hung the photo of Brecklyn in the living room today," I said.

"It was the first thing the kids pointed out when I got home from work," Abel said. He smiled at me then said, "I love having all the baby pictures on the wall together. It's hard to believe some of our kids were that small."

I swallowed. "I was thinking it would be nice to add a photo of Hope."

Abel's jaw clenched and I knew what he was going to say before the words left his mouth.

"No," he said firmly.

In the past, this is where the conversation had ended. This time, I pressed for more information. "Why not?"

"Seeing photos of Hope is emotionally painful," he said.

"I'm sure it is. I can't imagine your pain. Still, I think our kids should know they have a half-sister."

Abel squeezed the bridge of his nose. "I thought we agreed to start a new life together after we got married. I've tried hard to make you feel like number one."

"You've done a great job," I said. "But that's not the issue."

"Okay, explain it to me."

"I feel strongly there needs to be a photo of Hope somewhere in our home," I said. "There's something not right about having photos of our five kids but excluding her."

"I don't need a photo to remember Hope," Abel said, his voice rising slightly.

"I know that but the photo isn't just for you. It's for our children."

"How is it for our kids?"

"Krista and Hope are part of your history; they're part of our shared story. Sooner or later our kids are going to learn about them. I would rather they learn about your past from us, not someone else. I want them to feel that they can come to us about anything—good or bad. I don't want to ruin that trust when they discover that we've been hiding parts of our past from them."

Abel folded his arms and stared at his computer screen. I let the silence hang. I knew it was better to let him mull things over instead of pushing the issue. After a minute, Abel started writing again but his typing was slow and deliberate—a sign he couldn't focus.

I rolled on to my back and waited. The clickity clack of writing slowed even more then came to a complete stop. Abel lowered the lid to his laptop.

"I don't like any of Hope's photos," he said.

This was new information. In all our previous conversations Abel had only mentioned that the photos evoked strong emotions and memories. This was the first time he said anything about not liking them.

Abel continued, "In every photo she's hooked up to life support. There are tubes and wires connected to every part of her body. There isn't a single photograph of her without them."

I thought back to Hope's photo album. I had only looked through it once years earlier with Abel. I couldn't think of any pictures without her tiny body attached to life-saving equipment. Maybe if we looked again, we could find one he'd like.

"What about funeral photos?" I asked.

"What about them?"

"She wasn't on life support then. Maybe one of those would work."

Abel shook his head. "It was a closed-casket funeral. After her death an autopsy was performed and there were ugly scars that crisscrossed her skull. By the time we had the funeral, her hands and fingers had begun to shrivel and decay. I didn't want anyone seeing that. Besides, even if she looked presentable, a casket photo is too morbid to hang on our walls. I want a happy, healthy photo of Hope, like the ones of our kids on the wall, but those don't exist."

I didn't know what to say so I didn't say anything. At some point Abel opened his laptop and stared at the screen. The click of typing started and stopped in fits. I stared at the ceiling, wondering why I felt prompted to hang a photo of Hope. I still felt putting one up in our home was the right thing to do but didn't want the photo to be a source of contention or anguish.

At some point I realized Abel had stopped writing. Just as I was about to turn and look at him, he said, "There is one photograph of Hope I like."

I turned and got up on one elbow and waited for him to continue.

"It's one my dad took the first or second day in the hospital. Hope wasn't very active and I wanted a sign she was alive. I put her tiny hand around my index finger hoping she'd squeeze it the way babies do, but instead her hand rested on my finger. My dad was there with his camera and took a close-up of her hand."

"Is this photo in Hope's album?"

Abel thought for a moment. "Maybe. You can look if you want. If not, I'm sure my mom has a copy."

Abel returned to his writing.

I lay on my back and thought how I could incorporate a photo of Hope's hand into our home. Then I had an idea.

•••

"Hold still," I said to Aidan. I focused the camera on the football he held in his hands and snapped several photos with the digital camera. "Okay, you can move," I said.

Aidan looked over my shoulder as I browsed through the photographs on the camera's screen. Aidan had a tall and rectangular body like his father, and a fascination with screens and digital technology.

"Why are you taking photos of my hands?" he asked.

"It's a Christmas present for your dad," I said.

"Why does he want pictures of our hands?"

I don't know if he wants it, I thought but said, "You know how there are baby photos of you and your brothers and sisters on the living room wall?"

Aidan nodded.

"Well, I thought we could take photos of your hands and hang them on the wall too."

"Oh," Aidan said. "Can I play now?"

There were two good pictures to choose from. "Yes, go and play," I said.

Aidan sat next to his brother, Steven, who was crashing toy cars into each other on the floor.

"Your turn, Steven," I said.

Steven dropped the cars, pushed his long, blonde hair from his eyes, and hurried over.

"Do I get to hold a football?" he asked.

"You get a basketball," I said holding one out to him. I positioned the ball on his hip and placed his hand over it. "Don't move," I said and began taking photos.

"When is it my turn?" Molly asked from somewhere behind me.

"After Steven."

"I don't want to hold a ball."

"I know. There's a flower for you."

"A flower?" she said, her voice rising with excitement. "I love flowers."

I repositioned Steven's hand and took a few more photos. When it was Molly's turn, she flashed a big smile as she held a pink plastic flower, unaware that the camera was focused on her hands. Next it was Brennan's turn, who held his favorite action figure. Finally, it was Brecklyn's, our newborn's, turn. She was sleeping and I gently moved her from her crib to where the light was better. I was going to give her some beads to hold but the way she held her own hands would complement the photo of Hope holding Abel's finger. Before she could wake or stir, I took photo after photo of her tiny hands. It took the better part of an hour to take all the photos but as I scanned through them, I was happy with the results. I uploaded my favorite photos to a USB drive to give to a friend. Digital editing wasn't my strong suit but she was very adept and had agreed to help crop, size, and apply filters to the pictures I selected.

The only photo missing was Hope's. I had reached out to Abel's mom a few days earlier asking if she knew of the photo. She said she remembered it and would pass on a digital copy. I checked my email and was happy to see an unread email from her with an attachment. I opened it with eager anticipation: The photo was exactly as Abel remembered it: Hope's tiny fingers halfway curled around his index finger. Her hand looked so small in comparison to his. I compared that photo with those I had just taken. It would fit in nicely. I added Hope's photograph to the USB drive and prayed Abel would be receptive to this gift—one that I feared might be more for me and the kids than for him.

•••

A week before Christmas, the printed photos arrived in the mail. The entire project had been a lot of work but one I hoped Abel would treasure.

Molly wanted to help me wrap Dad's Christmas presents. Unfortunately, she'd helped the way most five-year-olds do: by getting in the way. I finally got her to hold out her hand so I could stick pieces of tape on each finger.

As I unrolled white wrapping paper with ice blue snowflakes and set out the two frames that each held three photos, Molly said, "There are six photos but we only have five kids. Who has two photos?"

"You all have one photo," I said. "The extra one is of your half-sister, Hope."

It felt strange talking about Hope without Abel in the room. He should be the one telling Molly about her other sibling.

"I have another sister?" Molly's face lit up. "Where is she? Can I play with her?"

I decided to answer her questions, hoping that when I told Abel about this conversation after Christmas, he would understand. "She's in Heaven," I said.

"She died?"

"Yes. You'll see her one day. Just not in this life."

"Oh," said Molly, clearly disappointed she didn't have another playmate. "But I can play with her in Heaven, right?"

"Yes," I said. "You can play with her in Heaven."

Molly seemed satisfied with my answers about her half-sister and I was happy we'd had the discussion. Maybe the photo would open more conversation with the rest of our kids. As I wrapped the presents, Molly asked questions about Santa Claus and how many days there were until Christmas. I took a piece of tape from one of her fingers and told her there were six days until Santa came.

...

I waited to give our presents to Abel as last of all the gifts on Christmas morning. I handed him the two presents as the kids played with their new toys amid piles of wrapping paper and boxes.

"What's this?" Abel said as I handed him two presents. "I thought we opened everything."

"These are for you."

"Who's it from?"

"All of us"

Abel opened the first present, which contained the hands of Molly, Brennan, and Brecklyn.

"Hands," he said. He looked at the next present and bit his lower lip as if sensing what was inside.

Slowly he opened the other present. I held my breath as he looked at the photos of Hope's, Aidan's, and Steven's hands. Tears rolled down his cheeks. He touched the photo of Hope's hand.

"You found the photo," he said.

"I want you to have photos of all your children."

"Thank you," he said giving me a hug. "This means the world to me."

Later that the afternoon we found a place for them on our wall above the piano. As the years passed, we added two more hands as another boy, Holden, and girl, Ette, completed our family.

As I expected, Hope's photo sparked questions and comments from our kids and the occasional eagle-eyed neighbor. As time passed, they've learned more about Abel's first marriage, about Krista's suicide, and their half-sister who died when she was nine days old. Sometimes they've asked questions that Abel and I can't answer. Will dad be married to you and Krista in Heaven? Why did Dad's first wife kill herself? Will Hope be a baby or an adult in the next life? To those questions we explain that there are some things we don't know yet; that we won't know until the next life. However, we tell them, the lack of answers shouldn't stop us from living.

"I don't know why I felt inspired to return to Utah after two years at the University of Puget Sound," I tell them when questions about following promptings or making decisions when we don't have answers arise. "I don't know who I would have married or what my life would look like if I had chosen to stop dating your father. I also don't know how Krista will fit in to our life together after we die but because of my choices, I have a wonderful family and a life that I wouldn't trade for anything."

And there are many things I *do* know. I know Abel and I won't be together in the next life unless we keep the vows and promises we made to each other when we were sealed in the temple. I know letting go of fear and worries when it comes to the unknown has freed me to live and enjoy my life and family. I know the wonderful promise that was made about all my children being in the temple together as a family will come true one day. I know Abel has a special place in his heart for Krista and Hope—and he always will. I know he loves me and together we've worked hard to build an eternal family. I know the happiness and joy in our marriage has surpassed all my expectations. And I know that however things turn out in the next life, as long as Abel and my children are there, I'll be happy.

ABOUT ABEL & JULIANNA

Abel and Julianna live in the heart of Utah with their seven children. Married for nineteen years, they continue to run together and build an eternal relationship. They look forward to spending the rest of this life and the eternities together. You can contact them at www.abelkeogh.com/contact.

2002   2022

ACKNOWLEDGEMENTS

Because of the personal nature of this story, *The Wife in the Next Life* was a project that took several years to write and revise. It would have been impossible to finish without help from the following individuals: Amy Paturel, Tristi Pinkston, Krista Isaacson, Trevor Howard, Carrie Westover, and Gracie Christensen. Thank you all for your comments, thoughts, insights, artistic talents, editing, and proofreading. Without your feedback and encouragement this story would still be lying dormant in our journals and partially completed chapters on our computers. Your help made it possible to share our story with the world.

OTHER BOOKS BY ABEL KEOGH

Memoirs
Room for Two

Dating Guides
Dating a Widower
The Ultimate Dating Guide for Widowers
Marrying a Widower
Life with a Widower

Novels
The Third
The Time Seller

Made in the USA
Monee, IL
26 November 2023